Grill It! Indoors

**Easy Recipes for Fast, Healthy
Electric Grilling.**

Compiled by Lesley Mackley

AN IMPRINT OF RUNNING PRESS
PHILADELPHIA · LONDON

2003 Salamander Books Ltd
Published by Salamander Books Ltd.
The Chrysalis Building, Bramley Road
London W10 6SP, United Kingdom

© Salamander Books Ltd. 2003

An imprint of **Chrysalis** Books Group plc

This edition published in the United States in 2003 by Courage Books, an imprint of
Running Press Book Publishers
125 South Twenty-second Street
Philadelphia, PA 19103-4399

3 5 7 9 8 6 4 2

Library of Congress Cataloging-in-Publication Number 2002110419
ISBN 0-7624-1490-1

Notice: The information contained in this book is true and complete to the best of our knowledge. All
recommendations are made without any guarantee on the part of the author or publisher. The author and
publisher disclaim all liability in connection with the use of this information.

Credits
Project Manager: Anne McDowall
Commissioning Editor: Stella Caldwell
Designer: Cara Hamilton
Production: Ian Hughes
Color reproduction: Anorax Imaging Ltd.
Printed in China

The recipes in this book have appeared in previous Salamander titles by other authors and have been edited
by Anne McDowall for this edition.

Notes
All spoon measurements are level: 1 teaspoon = 5ml spoon; 1 tablespoon = 15ml spoon
Cooking times given are approximate: they will vary according to the starting temperature of the food and
its thickness as well as the heat of the grill.
All recipes in this book assume that fish has been cleaned and scaled.

This book may be ordered from the publisher. But visit your bookstore first!
Visit us on the web!
www.runningpress.com

Contents

Introduction 6

Appetizers and Snacks 11

Fish 23

Poultry 39

Meat 55

Vegetarian Dishes 79

Fruit 91

Index 96

Introduction

We have been grilling food ever since man first discovered how to make a fire and then cooked meat over it. Today there are many reasons why grilling—cooking by direct exposure to radiant heat—is still one of our favorite methods of cooking food. It is a healthier option than frying or roasting, as it produces food that is lower in fat, and it is quick and easy, requiring no sophisticated cooking skills. Grilling also gives a wonderful flavor, as the natural sugars in the food caramelize on the surface. This also has the effect of producing an attractive color that is very appealing.

Types of indoor grills
Cooking over hot coals is the simplest form of grilling, but it is not always practical and it is certainly not a year-round option for most of us. There are, however, a variety of ways of grilling indoors.

Broilers
Most traditional domestic ovens have an integral broiler, which cooks with heat from above. However, the food is not in direct contact with the heat so it is not sealed as efficiently as it is on a ridged stovetop grillpan or in a grilling machine. For the best results, broilers should be preheated so that they are as hot as possible when the food is placed under them. Larger range-style stoves often have a griddle plate included on the burner and this may be reversible, with ridges on one side and a flat surface on the other.

Stovetop griddles
These are generally either made in cast iron or cast aluminum, both of which give a very even heat. Some are enameled or have a nonstick coating. The nonstick pans are easier to clean but the cast iron ones build up a patina, which, over time, produces a durable nonstick surface. Some users find that these grills can produce smoke, but this can be prevented by not having the heat too high and avoiding the use of excess oil. Because the surface of the food is completely sealed, it will remain moist and juicy inside and there will be very little shrinkage or loss of nutrients and flavor. Any fat collects in the channels and can be poured away or mopped up with paper towels.

Indoor electric grills
These are the nearest thing to cooking outdoors and they can be used anywhere there is access to an electric power point. The food is placed on nonstick metal bars and the fat drips through to a pan underneath. Some also have a flat area, which is very useful for cooking eggs if you are preparing a large breakfast. Most have a variable heat control. Removable grill plates and pan make for easy cleaning. Some models have a glass lid and although this eliminates smoke and reduces any splattering, the food tends to steam when covered in this way.

Electric grilling machines
Increasingly popular, electric grilling machines or contact grills have a hinged lid, which closes over the food, searing the meat and locking in the juices, while enabling both sides to be cooked at once. This significantly reduces the cooking time and also eliminates smoke. The grilling surface is tilted to allow any fat to drain off into a drip tray. Grilling machines are easy to clean due to a nonstick coating and some have removable grill plates. A useful feature on some models is that the two halves of the machine can be opened out to give twice the surface, enabling it to be used like a conventional grill. It may also have a lid that contains a compartment in which buns, bread

Choosing a grill

	Grilling machine	Electric grill	Stovetop grillpan	Broiler
Self contained – can be used anywhere	✓	✓	✗	✗
Thermostatic control	✓	✓	✗	✗
Chargrill effect	✓	✓	✓	✗
Low-fat cooking	✓	✓	✓	✓
Cover to eliminate smoke	✓	✓	✗	✗
Contact on both sides for quick cooking	✓	✗	✗	✗
Direct contact to seal food	✓	✓	✓	✗

and tortillas may be warmed for serving with burgers and other grilled food.

Grilling machines come in a variety of sizes. The smallest is ideal for one or two people while the medium-size model is suitable for a family or for entertaining. Party-size grilling machines are perfect for larger gatherings and, as they can be fitted onto a cart, they can be wheeled into the dining room or used out in the garden for fuss-free barbecues. For many of the recipes in this book, the medium-size model would be the most practical. If using the small model, you may need to cook food in batches, keeping food warm in a low oven until everything is cooked.

Cooking in a grilling machine
The hinged lid of a grilling machine is loose enough for it to accommodate food up to 1 inch thick. For best results, however, make sure that the food to be cooked is of an even thickness in order to ensure good contact with the grilling surface. Chicken drumsticks and thick pork ribs are not suitable for cooking in this type of grill, and the different ingredients on a kabob skewer should be cut so that they are all the same size. Kabobs should be cooked on wooden skewers.

Cooking times depend on the type of food, its density and thickness. The instruction book provided with the machine will contain a chart of cooking times, but they are only a guide, so it is important to check that the food is thoroughly cooked before serving. The times given are for fresh or fully defrosted ingredients.

As food cooks so quickly in the grilling machine, it is important to have any accompaniments and garnishes ready before you start cooking. Bread, burger buns, pita bread, and tortillas can all be warmed in the bun warmer while the main dish is being grilled.

Food suitable for grilling
An enormous variety of food is ideal for grilling. The main point to remember is that it is a very quick way of cooking, so choose ingredients with that in mind. Meat for grilling should be the cuts that are lean and tender. Tougher cuts, which require long slow cooking in order to become tender, would not be suitable. Poultry and fish all cook beautifully and the grill gives a wonderful flavor to vegetables and even fruit. Bread toasted on the grill has a delicious chargrilled taste, making it perfect for crostini and bruschetta.

It is very important to make sure that the food is as dry as possible before placing it on the grill. Allow marinades to run off, or pat food dry with paper towels.

Grilling is a very healthy low-fat way of cooking, but if you are cooking an ingredient that contains very little or no fat, a little oil brushed or sprayed onto the cooking plates before cooking will prevent it from drying out.

With stovetop and electric indoor grills, do not be tempted to turn the food too quickly. Leave whatever is being cooked on the grill for long enough to allow the underside to become sealed and for attractive grid lines to form before turning. If it is moved too soon, this will not happen.

Meat and poultry should be cooked until the juices run clear, and fish until the flesh is opaque. It is particularly important, for safely reasons, to ensure that poultry and meat are thoroughly cooked. The best way to check this is with a meat thermometer, but if you do not have one, the following test will give you a reasonably accurate indication of the internal temperature of meat. Insert a metal skewer into the thickest part of the meat and count to 30. Remove the skewer and place it on the outside of your wrist. If the skewer is warm the meat is still rare; if quite hot, the meat is medium rare, and if the skewer is very hot indeed, the meat is quite well done.

Tips for grilling

Whatever type of grill you are using, it should be preheated before use. Broilers should be as hot as possible before the food is placed under them and the heat can be reduced once the food starts to brown. A stovetop grill needs to be heated for a minute or two and the best way to determine when it is ready is to sprinkle a little water on the surface. If the water sizzles immediately, the grill plate is hot enough. Indoor grills and grilling machines also require preheating. An indicator light on the grilling machine will be visible while it is heating up and goes out when the machine is ready to use.

Food suitable for grilling

Lamb—chops, kabobs, burgers, steaks

Pork—steaks, kabobs, sausages, ham steaks, bacon

Beef—steaks, burgers, kabobs, sausages

Seafood—fish fillets and steaks, kabobs, scallops, shrimp

Poultry and game—chicken and turkey fillets, chicken thighs, chicken and turkey burgers, kabobs, venison steaks, burgers and sausages

Vegetables—asparagus, eggplant, zucchini, bell peppers, sliced potatoes, fennel, squash, corn, onions, mushrooms, artichokes

Fruit—apples, pears, peaches, pineapple rings, bananas, figs

Bread—slices of baguette and ciabatta, sandwiches

Polenta, Tofu, Halloumi cheese

Marinades and sauces

Most food will benefit from being marinated before grilling. The oil in a marinade helps to keep it moist, and vinegar or citrus juice tenderizes meat. Herbs and spices give extra flavor. Marinating should not just be confined to meat or fish, as vegetables are particularly delicious after spending some time in an herby marinade. If you do not have time to leave food in a marinade for a few hours or overnight, even marinating for a short time will make a difference to the flavor of the food. Allow the marinated food to come to room temperature before grilling, and when you remove it from the marinade, allow the excess to run off, or even pat it dry with paper towels. If the food is too wet it will not grill successfully. Many of the recipes in this book include marinades, but a few other tasty and easy-to-prepare ones are given below.

As grilled food can be dry and crisp, it is always enhanced if served with a sauce. Many of the recipes in this book include sauces, but when time is short just a squeeze of lemon juice on fish, a spoonful of yogurt with a Middle-Eastern inspired kabob, or some ready-made mayonnaise with grilled shrimp or chicken will make all the difference. Salsas are a cross between a salad and a sauce and are quick and easy to make. A simple tomato salsa consisting of chopped tomato, onion and chile will give a kick to the simplest grilled dishes and a mango salsa adds a sweet and sour flavor to Caribbean or Cajun-style food.

To make these marinades (shown here clockwise from top left), simply combine all ingredients in a bowl. Use as required.

Tandoori marinade
½ cup thin plain yogurt
2 teaspoons garam masala
1 teaspoon ground cumin
½ teaspoon chili powder
½ teaspoon turmeric
3 tablespoons chopped fresh mint

Tangy marinade
¾ cup grapeseed oil
Grated zest and juice 1 lime
3 tablespoons finely chopped cilantro

Lemon marinade
¾ cup sunflower oil
Grated zest and juice 1 small lemon
½ teaspoon cracked black pepper
2 tablespoons chopped fresh dill

Mediterranean marinade
¾ cup olive oil
1 tablespoon sundried tomato paste
2 garlic cloves, crushed
1 teaspoon chopped fresh oregano
1 tablespoon chopped fresh thyme

Chinese marinade
1 tablespoon sesame oil
3 tablespoons sunflower oil
¼ cup soy sauce
2 tablespoons clear honey
2 teaspoons Chinese five-spice powder
2 garlic cloves, crushed
1 stalk lemongrass, finely chopped

Appetizers and Snacks

Grilled Yellow Bell Pepper Soup

6 YELLOW BELL PEPPERS

4 MEDIUM LEEKS, WHITE AND PALE GREEN PARTS ONLY, THINLY SLICED

2 TABLESPOONS OLIVE OIL

3 CUPS CHICKEN STOCK

SALT AND GROUND BLACK PEPPER

TOASTED COUNTRY BREAD, TO SERVE

◆ Quarter bell peppers lengthwise. Place in the grilling machine and grill 8 to 10 minutes until beginning to blacken. Alternatively, preheat a grill and cook, skin side up until beginning to blacken. Place peppers in a plastic bag, closing tightly and leave 10 minutes.

◆ Meanwhile, place sliced leeks in a bowl of cold water to soak 5 minutes. Drain.

◆ Remove peppers from plastic bag and scrape off and discard skins. Roughly chop flesh.

◆ In a large saucepan, heat oil, add leeks and cook gently 10 minutes until soft but not colored.

◆ Add peppers and stock and season with salt and pepper. Bring to a boil, then turn down the heat and simmer 20 minutes.

◆ Purée in a blender, then pass through a strainer into the rinsed-out pan. Reheat, taste, and season. Serve with toasted country bread.

Greek Peach and Grilled Green Bell Pepper Salad

MAKES 4 SERVINGS

4 GREEN BELL PEPPERS

2 LARGE RIPE PEACHES

6 OUNCES FETA CHEESE

12 CALAMATA OLIVES

CUMIN DRESSING

2 TEASPOONS CUMIN SEEDS

½ CUP OLIVE OIL

3 TABLESPOONS WHITE WINE VINEGAR

SALT AND GROUND BLACK PEPPER

PINCH SUGAR

◆ Quarter bell peppers lengthwise and remove cores and seeds. Place peppers in the grilling machine and grill 8 to 10 minutes until beginning to blacken. Alternatively, preheat a grill and cook, skin side up.

◆ Remove peppers and place in a plastic bag, closing tightly. Leave 10 minutes. Once cool, peel off blackened skins and discard. Slice flesh into thick strips.

◆ Halve and pit peaches and slice flesh thickly. Cut feta into small cubes. Place peppers, peaches, feta, and olives in a mixing bowl.

◆ To make dressing, dry-roast cumin seeds in a skillet about 1 minute until they begin to pop and their aroma is released.

◆ Place olive oil, wine vinegar, salt, pepper, and sugar in a bowl and add roasted cumin seeds. Stir to combine.

◆ Pour dressing over salad ingredients and toss gently. Refrigerate 1 hour before serving.

Bell Pepper and Anchovy Salad

MAKES 6 SERVINGS

3 LARGE RED BELL PEPPERS

3 LARGE YELLOW BELL PEPPERS

⅓ CUP OLIVE OIL OR OLIVE AND SUNFLOWER OIL MIXED

1 TABLESPOON WINE OR BALSAMIC VINEGAR

SALT AND GROUND BLACK PEPPER

2-OUNCE CAN ANCHOVIES, DRAINED, RINSED, AND CHOPPED

1 CUP BLACK OLIVES, PITTED

3 OR 4 TABLESPOONS CHOPPED FRESH PARSLEY

2 HARD-BOILED EGGS

◆ Quarter bell peppers lengthwise and remove cores and seeds. Place peppers in the grilling machine and grill 8 to 10 minutes until beginning to blacken. Alternatively, preheat a grill and cook, skin side up until beginning to blacken.

◆ Remove peppers from grilling machine or grill and place in a plastic bag, closing tightly. Leave 10 minutes. Remove peppers from bag and scrape off skins. Cut flesh into wide strips.

◆ Put oil, vinegar, salt, pepper, anchovies, olives, and parsley into a large bowl and mix well. Add peppers and toss to coat thoroughly.

◆ Halve eggs and remove yolks. Roughly chop whites and sprinkle over peppers. Chop egg yolks finely and sprinkle over whites. Chill salad before serving.

Eggplant and Mushroom Satay

MAKES 4 SERVINGS

18 CHESTNUT MUSHROOMS, WIPED

1 LARGE EGGPLANT, WEIGHING ABOUT 12 OUNCES

OIL FOR BRUSHING

CHINESE CABBAGE, SHREDDED, TO SERVE

½ SMALL CUCUMBER, CUT INTO MATCHSTICK STRIPS, TO SERVE

2 TABLESPOONS FINELY CHOPPED CILANTRO, TO GARNISH

MARINADE

⅓ CUP OLIVE OIL

3 TABLESPOONS SOY SAUCE

1 TABLESPOON WINE VINEGAR

1 GARLIC CLOVE, CRUSHED

SALT AND GROUND BLACK PEPPER

SATAY SAUCE

¼ CUP SMOOTH PEANUT BUTTER

⅔ CUP COCONUT MILK

2 TEASPOONS THAI RED CURRY PASTE

1 TABLESPOON THAI FISH SAUCE

1 TABLESPOON SOFT BROWN SUGAR

◆ Cut mushrooms in half. Cut eggplant into ¾-inch slices, then cut each slice into 4 segments. Place vegetables in a shallow dish.

◆ To make marinade, in a small bowl, mix together olive oil, soy sauce, wine vinegar, garlic, salt, and pepper.

◆ Spoon marinade over vegetables, making sure they are thoroughly coated. Leave at least 1 hour, turning occasionally.

◆ To make satay sauce, mix together peanut butter, coconut milk, red curry paste, fish sauce and sugar and set aside.

◆ Thread pieces of mushroom and eggplant alternately onto 12 skewers and brush with oil. Place in the grilling machine and grill 5 or 6 minutes. Alternatively, cook on a preheated grill about 10 minutes, turning frequently and brushing with oil, until browned.

◆ Place vegetables on a bed of Chinese cabbage and cucumber strips. Sprinkle with cilantro and serve immediately, with satay sauce.

Tomato Bruschetta

*9 OUNCES MOZZARELLA,
CUT INTO SMALL CUBES*

20 RIPE CHERRY TOMATOES, QUARTERED

3 TABLESPOONS OLIVE OIL

*1 TEASPOON BALSAMIC OR
SHERRY VINEGAR*

SALT AND GROUND BLACK PEPPER

6 THICK SLICES COUNTRY BREAD

2 GARLIC CLOVES, PEELED

4 OUNCES ARUGULA OR WATERCRESS

*GENEROUS HANDFUL FRESH BASIL LEAVES,
TO GARNISH*

◆ Place mozzarella in a bowl with tomatoes. Whisk together olive oil and vinegar, season with salt and pepper, and pour over Mozzarella cheese and tomatoes. Mix well.

◆ Place bread in the grilling machine and grill 5 minutes until toasted. Alternatively, preheat a grill and toast bread on both sides.

◆ Cut garlic cloves in half and rub each slice of toasted bread with a cut side of garlic clove.

◆ Place a slice of toast on each of 6 plates and surround each slice with arugula or watercress. Pile mozzarella and tomato mixture on top of toast, garnish with basil leaves, and serve.

Reuben Sandwiches

MAKES 4 SERVINGS

½ STICK BUTTER

8 SLICES LIGHT RYE BREAD WITH
CARAWAY SEEDS

8 OUNCES SLICED CORNED BEEF

1 CUP SAUERKRAUT

¼ CUP THOUSAND ISLAND OR
RUSSIAN DRESSING

8 SLICES SWISS CHEESE
(E.G. GRUYÈRE OR EMMENTHAL)

FRENCH FRIES, TO SERVE (OPTIONAL)

◆ Lightly butter each slice of bread on one side. Arrange half the salt beef on the unbuttered side of 4 slices of bread.

◆ Top each slice with one-quarter of the sauerkraut and 1 tablespoon of Thousand Island or Russian dressing.

◆ Place 2 slices of cheese on each sandwich and finish with remaining salt beef. Cover with remaining slices of bread, buttered side out.

◆ Place 2 assembled sandwiches in the grilling machine and grill 6 or 7 minutes until golden and crisp. Alternatively, preheat a grill and cook sandwiches 3 to 5 minutes on each side.

◆ Repeat the cooking process for 2 remaining sandwiches. Serve reuben sandwiches while still hot, with French fries if desired.

Steak Sandwiches with Red Onion Relish

MAKES 4 SERVINGS

4 VERY THIN SANDWICH STEAKS

OLIVE OIL FOR BRUSHING

STEAK SEASONING

8 THICK SLICES WHITE BREAD

FRENCH FRIES, TO SERVE (OPTIONAL)

RED ONION RELISH

2 TABLESPOONS OLIVE OIL

2 RED ONIONS, SLICED

1 TABLESPOON BROWN SUGAR

2 TABLESPOONS RED WINE VINEGAR

SMALL PIECE BUTTER

◆ To prepare relish, heat olive oil in a skillet. Add onions and cook gently 15 to 20 minutes until onions are tender.

◆ Pour in ⅔ cup water, add brown sugar and vinegar, and simmer until almost all liquid has evaporated and onions are tender. Stir in butter and set aside (this relish is best served warm).

◆ Brush steaks with oil and season with a little steak seasoning. Place in the grilling machine and grill 4 or 5 minutes. Keep warm. Alternatively, place steaks on a hot grill and cook 2 or 3 minutes on each side.

◆ Place bread in the grilling machine and grill 4 or 5 minutes, or place on the grill and toast lightly.

◆ Place a cooked steak on each of 4 toasted bread slices. Top with relish and cover with remaining toasted bread. Serve at once while still hot, accompanied by French fries, if desired.

Mediterranean Chicken Sandwiches

MAKES 4 SERVINGS

4 SMALL SKINLESS CHICKEN FILLETS

2 GARLIC CLOVES, CRUSHED

2 TABLESPOONS OLIVE OIL

1 TEASPOON DRIED MEDITERRANEAN HERBS

SALT AND GROUND BLACK PEPPER

3 TABLESPOONS PLAIN OR GARLIC MAYONNAISE

8 SLICES SUN-DRIED TOMATO BREAD

2 LARGE PLUM TOMATOES, SLICED

HANDFUL FRESH BASIL LEAVES

CHERRY TOMATOES, TO SERVE (OPTIONAL)

◆ Carefully cut chicken fillets in half horizontally to make 8 thin slices. Transfer to a shallow glass or ceramic dish.

◆ Mix garlic, olive oil, herbs, and salt and pepper together in a small bowl. Pour over chicken, tossing to coat well. Cover with plastic wrap and let marinate 1 hour.

◆ Lift chicken slices from the dish, place in the grilling machine and grill 4 or 5 minutes. Alternatively, cook on a preheated grill 2 or 3 minutes on each side until golden. Remove from heat.

◆ Spread mayonnaise on 4 slices of bread. Arrange tomato slices on bread and top each slice with 2 pieces of chicken. Season with salt and pepper and sprinkle with a few basil leaves. Cover with remaining bread and serve, accompanied by tomato salad, if desired.

Grilled Prosciutto and Figs

MAKES 4 SERVINGS

8 FRESH RIPE FIGS

3 TABLESPOONS OLIVE OIL

*12 THIN SLICES PROSCIUTTO OR
PARMA HAM*

*3 TABLESPOONS FRESHLY GRATED
PARMESAN CHEESE*

CRUSHED BLACK PEPPER, TO SERVE

◆ Take each fig and stand it upright. Using a sharp kitchen knife, make 2 cuts across and downward in each fig, not quite quartering it but keeping it intact. Ease figs open and brush with olive oil.

◆ Place figs in the grilling machine and grill 5 minutes until hot and golden brown. Alternatively, preheat a grill and cook figs, cut side up, until browning and hot through. Keep warm.

◆ Place prosciutto slices in the grilling machine, or on a grill, and cook 2 or 3 minutes until starting to crisp.

◆ Arrange 3 pieces of ham and 2 figs per person on warm plates. Sprinkle with grated Parmesan and season with plenty of crushed black pepper. Serve at once.

Fragrant Chicken Kabobs

MAKES ABOUT 20

*14 OUNCES CHICKEN FILLET,
CUT INTO THIN STRIPS*

2 GARLIC CLOVES, CRUSHED

*1 FRESH RED CHILE, SEEDED
AND CHOPPED*

2 PINCHES SAFFRON THREADS

¼ CUP OLIVE OIL

SALT

HANDFUL MINT LEAVES

JUICE 1 LARGE LEMON

◆ Place chicken strips in a shallow nonmetallic dish. Put garlic, chile, saffron, olive oil, salt, and most of the mint and lemon juice into a blender. Mix to a purée. Pour over chicken, turn to coat in purée, and let marinate 30 minutes.

◆ Thread chicken onto skewers. Place in the grilling machine and grill 7 or 8 minutes until golden and cooked through. Alternatively, preheat a grill and cook kabobs 3 or 4 minutes on each side.

◆ Mix remaining mint and lemon juice together and sprinkle over chicken just before serving.

Grilled Vegetable Salad with Skordalià

2 YELLOW OR RED BELL PEPPERS, SEEDED AND QUARTERED

8 OUNCES RAW BEET, SCRUBBED AND THINLY SLICED

8 OUNCES JERUSALEM ARTICHOKES, SCRUBBED AND THINLY SLICED

1 EGGPLANT, THINLY SLICED

2 SMALL ZUCCHINI, SLICED LENGTHWISE

1 SMALL HEAD RADICCHIO, CUT INTO THIN WEDGES

8 OUNCES ASPARAGUS SPEARS, TRIMMED

¼ CUP LEMON CITRUS OIL (SEE NOTE)

SKORDALIÀ

2 SLICES DAY-OLD WHITE BREAD, CUBED

¼ CUP MILK

2 GARLIC CLOVES, CRUSHED

½ TEASPOON SALT

PINCH CAYENNE

⅓ CUP EXTRA VIRGIN OLIVE OIL

1 TABLESPOON LEMON JUICE

◆ To make skordalià, soak bread in milk 5 minutes. Squeeze out milk and put bread in a blender or food processor. Add garlic, sea salt, and cayenne and blend until smooth.

◆ Gradually blend in oil and 1 tablespoon boiling water to form a thick sauce. Stir in lemon juice and season to taste.

◆ Brush all vegetables with citrus oil and grill each vegetable separately in the grilling machine until browned and tender. (Cooking times will vary depending on the vegetable.) Alternatively, preheat a grill, place vegetables on a baking tray, and cook until tender.

◆ Arrange vegetables on a large platter and drizzle over any remaining oil. Serve at room temperature with skordalià.

Note: To make lemon citrus oil, place 4 strips of lemon peel in a clean jar and add 1¼ cups extra virgin olive oil. Store in a cool, dark place up to 2 weeks, strain into a clean jar, and use as required.

Fish

Fresh Tuna and Bean Salad

MAKES 4 SERVINGS

2 FRESH TUNA STEAKS, EACH WEIGHING
ABOUT 8 OUNCES

3 TABLESPOONS OLIVE OIL

1 GARLIC CLOVE, CRUSHED

14-OUNCE CAN FLAGEOLET OR
KIDNEY BEANS, DRAINED

1 RED ONION, THINLY SLICED

2 RIPE PLUM TOMATOES, PEELED,
SEEDED, AND DICED

2 TABLESPOONS CHOPPED
FRESH PARSLEY

1 TABLESPOON CHOPPED
FRESH BASIL

2 TEASPOONS BALSAMIC VINEGAR

SALT AND GROUND BLACK PEPPER

4 OUNCES ARUGULA

◆ Brush tuna steaks with a little olive oil, then place in the grilling machine and grill 6 to 8 minutes. Alternatively, place on a grill and cook 4 or 5 minutes on each side. Remove fish and let cool.

◆ Break tuna into large chunks and place in a large bowl. Gently stir in garlic, beans, onion, tomatoes, parsley, and basil.

◆ In a small bowl, blend remaining oil with vinegar and salt and pepper. Pour over salad, toss well, and let marinate 1 hour.

◆ Stir in arugula leaves and serve at once.

Tiger Shrimp with Cilantro Mayonnaise

½ CUP SWEET CHILI SAUCE

¼ CUP TOMATO PASTE

4 TEASPOONS LEMON JUICE

4 GARLIC CLOVES, CRUSHED

4 TEASPOONS SESAME OIL

16 RAW UNPEELED TIGER SHRIMP

CILANTRO MAYONNAISE

⅓ CUP MAYONNAISE

½ FRESH RED CHILE, SEEDED AND FINELY CHOPPED

½ SMALL RED ONION, FINELY CHOPPED

2 TABLESPOONS CHOPPED CILANTRO

2 TABLESPOONS LEMON JUICE

◆ To make marinade, combine sweet chili sauce, tomato paste, lemon juice, garlic, and sesame oil in a large bowl.

◆ Add shrimp to bowl of marinade and toss to coat evenly. Cover and refrigerate 2 hours, if time permits.

◆ To make cilantro mayonnaise, mix together mayonnaise, chile, onion, cilantro, and lemon juice. Season to taste with salt and pepper. Cover and refrigerate until required.

◆ Thread 4 shrimp onto each skewer, place in the grilling machine, and grill 4 or 5 minutes until pink. Alternatively, preheat a grill and cook shrimp 4 or 5 minutes on each side.

◆ Serve shrimp hot, on or off skewers, with cilantro mayonnaise.

Asian Squid and Scallop Salad

MAKES 4 SERVINGS

8 LARGE SCALLOPS

VEGETABLE OIL FOR BRUSHING

12 CLEANED BABY SQUID

2 GREEN ONIONS

1 STARFRUIT

6 OUNCES CHINESE CABBAGE

¼ CUP TORN CILANTRO LEAVES

CILANTRO SPRIGS, TO GARNISH

LEMONGRASS DRESSING

1 SMALL STALK LEMONGRASS,
VERY FINELY CHOPPED

3 TABLESPOONS PEANUT OIL

1½ TABLESPOONS SOY SAUCE

1½ TABLESPOONS LEMON JUICE

2 TEASPOONS SESAME OIL

1½ TEASPOONS CLEAR HONEY

1 LARGE GARLIC CLOVE, CRUSHED

◆ To make dressing, place lemongrass, peanut oil, soy sauce, lemon juice, sesame oil, honey, and garlic in a screw-top jar and shake well to combine. Set aside.

◆ Brush scallops with a little oil and place in the grilling machine. Grill 4 to 6 minutes. Place squid in the grilling machine and grill 2 minutes.

◆ Alternatively, preheat a grill and cook scallops 4 or 5 minutes on each side and squid about 1 minute on each side.

◆ Slice green onions on the diagonal and cut starfruit into thin slices. Wash Chinese cabbage and shred coarsely. Toss cilantro leaves with cabbage and divide between 4 plates.

◆ Arrange seafood on plates with green onions and starfruit. Spoon dressing over each salad and serve at once.

Red Mullet with Fennel

MAKES 4 SERVINGS

¼ CUP OLIVE OIL

1 TEASPOON LEMON JUICE

1 TEASPOON FENNEL SEEDS

¼ TEASPOON EACH SEA SALT AND PEPPER

4 RED MULLET, EACH WEIGHING
ABOUT 8 OUNCES

FRESH FENNEL LEAVES, TO GARNISH

◆ In a large shallow dish mix together olive oil, lemon juice, fennel seeds, sea salt, and pepper.

◆ Scrape away hard scales, remove gills and fins and clean inside of fish, but leave liver. Rinse, drain, and wipe fish dry with absorbent kitchen paper. Place in marinade and leave 1 hour, basting occasionally.

◆ Drain fish and place in the grilling machine. Grill 6 to 8 minutes. Alternatively, cook mullet on a preheated grill 4 or 5 minutes on each side. Garnish with fennel leaves to serve.

Cod with Teriyaki Glaze

MAKES 4 SERVINGS

4 COD FILLETS WITH SKIN

CHERVIL SPRIGS, TO GARNISH

*STIR-FRIED VEGETABLES, TO SERVE
(OPTIONAL)*

TERIYAKI GLAZE

2 TABLESPOONS SOY SAUCE

*1 TABLESPOON RICE WINE OR
MEDIUM-DRY SHERRY*

1 TABLESPOON LIGHT SOFT BROWN SUGAR

1 TEASPOON GRATED FRESH GINGER

◆ To make teriyaki glaze, gently heat together soy sauce, rice wine or sherry, sugar, and ginger 2 or 3 minutes in a small saucepan until lightly syrupy. Let cool.

◆ Brush both sides of fish fillets with teriyaki glaze. Place in the grilling machine and grill 3 to 5 minutes. Alternatively, cook fish on a preheated grill 3 or 4 minutes on each side.

◆ Transfer fish to warm serving plates. Reheat any remaining glaze and pour over fish. Garnish with chervil sprigs and serve with stir-fried vegetables, if desired.

Red Snapper with Tarragon

MAKES 4 SERVINGS

2 TABLESPOONS WHITE WINE VINEGAR

1½ TO 2 TEASPOONS DIJON-STYLE MUSTARD

1 SMALL SHALLOT, FINELY CHOPPED

1 GARLIC CLOVE, FINELY CRUSHED

½ CUP OLIVE OIL, PLUS EXTRA FOR BRUSHING

14 OUNCES TOMATOES, PEELED, SEEDED, AND DICED

1½ TABLESPOONS CHOPPED FRESH TARRAGON

2 TABLESPOONS FINELY CHOPPED FRESH CHIVES

SALT AND PEPPER

PINCH SUGAR (OPTIONAL)

4 RED SNAPPER, EACH WEIGHING ABOUT 10 OUNCES, SCALED

4 SPRIGS TARRAGON

TARRAGON SPRIGS AND LIME WEDGES, TO GARNISH

◆ Whisk together vinegar, mustard, shallot, and garlic until mixture is emulsified, then gradually whisk in oil.

◆ Add tomatoes, tarragon, and chives and season with salt and pepper. Add a pinch of sugar, if desired, then let stand 30 to 60 minutes.

◆ With the point of a sharp knife, cut 2 slashes on both sides of each fish. Season fish and stuff a tarragon sprig in each cavity.

◆ Brush with oil, then place in the grilling machine and grill about 8 to 10 minutes. Alternatively, cook on a preheated grill about 10 minutes, turning and brushing with oil once.

◆ Transfer cooked fish to serving plates. Stir tomato mixture, spoon some onto fish, and serve remainder separately. Garnish fish with sprigs of tarragon and lime wedges to serve.

Tandoori Fish Kabobs

2 FLOUNDER, SKINNED AND FILLETED

16 LARGE RAW SHRIMP,
PEELED AND DEVEINED

1 POUND COD FILLET, SKINNED AND DICED

1 SMALL ONION, VERY FINELY CHOPPED

2 GARLIC CLOVES, CRUSHED

1 TEASPOON GRATED FRESH GINGER

1 TEASPOON MILD CURRY POWDER

1 TEASPOON PAPRIKA

1/4 TEASPOON CHILI POWDER

1/4 TEASPOON TURMERIC

1 TABLESPOON LEMON JUICE

2/3 CUP PLAIN YOGURT

2 LIMES, CUT INTO WEDGES

GREEN SALAD AND NAAN BREAD,
TO SERVE (OPTIONAL)

◆ Wash and dry flounder fillets. Cut each one in half lengthwise to make 16 thin strips of fish. Roll up and secure with toothpicks. Place in a shallow dish with shrimp and diced cod.

◆ To make marinade, in a bowl mix together onion, garlic, ginger, curry powder, paprika, chili powder, turmeric, lemon juice, yogurt, and salt and pepper.

◆ Pour marinade over seafood. Cover and marinate 30 minutes.

◆ Thread fish, shrimp, and lime wedges alternately onto skewers. Place in the grilling machine and grill about 8 to 10 minutes, until cooked through. Alternatively, cook kabobs on a preheated grill 8 minutes, turning occasionally.

◆ Place two kabobs on each plate. Serve with a green salad and naan bread and garnish with extra lime wedges, if desired.

Chinese-style Salmon Steaks

2 TABLESPOONS HOISIN SAUCE

2 TABLESPOONS DARK SOY SAUCE

1 TEASPOON SESAME OIL

1/4 TEASPOON FIVE-SPICE POWDER

2 TEASPOONS CLEAR HONEY

1 GARLIC CLOVE, CRUSHED

1 TEASPOON GRATED FRESH GINGER

4 SALMON STEAKS, EACH WEIGHING
ABOUT 5 OUNCES, WASHED AND DRIED

◆ In a bowl mix together hoisin sauce, soy sauce, sesame oil, five-spice powder, honey, garlic, and ginger.

◆ Brush each salmon steak with glaze. Place in the grilling machine and grill 6 to 8 minutes until golden and cooked through.

◆ Alternatively, preheat a grill and cook salmon steaks 3 or 4 minutes on each side, basting with remaining glaze.

◆ Serve at once, with a green salad and garlic bread if desired.

Scallop and Parma Ham Kabobs

MAKES 4 SERVINGS

20 *LARGE FRESH SCALLOPS*

10 *THIN SLICES PARMA HAM*

20 *LARGE SAGE LEAVES*

2 *TABLESPOONS CHOPPED FRESH CHERVIL*

1 *TEASPOON FENNEL SEEDS, TOASTED AND CRUSHED*

2 *SPRIGS ROSEMARY*

⅔ *CUP WHITE WINE*

¼ *CUP HAZELNUT OIL*

SELECTION OF SALAD LEAVES, TO SERVE

SALSA

1 *RIPE MANGO, PEELED, PITTED AND DICED*

2 *RIPE TOMATOES, PEELED, SEEDED, AND DICED*

1 *FRESH GREEN CHILE, SEEDED AND DICED*

2 *TABLESPOONS CHOPPED FRESH CHERVIL*

½ *RED ONION, FINELY CHOPPED*

JUICE 1 *LIME*

2 *TABLESPOONS HAZELNUT OIL*

½ *TEASPOON SUGAR*

SALT AND PEPPER

◆ Wash scallops. Cut away tough grey membrane from each one and discard. Pat dry. Cut each slice of Parma ham in half lengthwise to form 20 long thin strips.

◆ Wrap a sage leaf then a strip of ham around each scallop to form small packages. Place carefully in a shallow dish.

◆ To make marinade, in a small bowl combine chervil, fennel seeds, rosemary, wine, and hazelnut oil. Pour over kabobs, cover dish, and let marinate 2 hours.

◆ To make salsa, in a bowl combine mango, tomatoes, chile, chervil, red onion, lime juice, hazelnut oil, and sugar. Season to taste with salt and pepper and set aside to allow flavors to infuse.

◆ Remove scallop packages from marinade, thread onto skewers, and place in the grilling machine. Grill 4 to 6 minutes until firm. Alternatively, cook on a preheated grill 2 or 3 minutes on each side.

◆ Serve kabobs at once, with a little salsa and a selection of salad leaves.

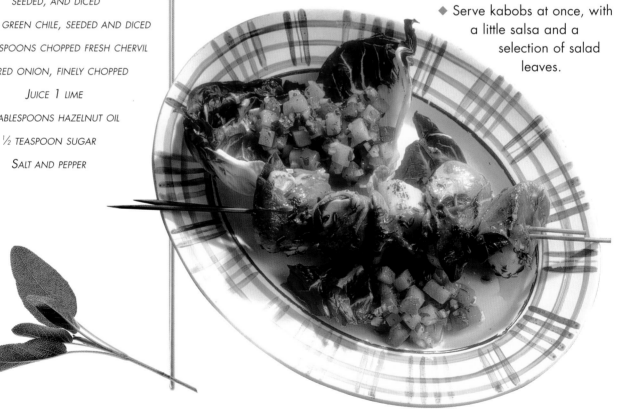

Skewered Tuna Rolls

MAKES 4 SERVINGS

1½ POUNDS FRESH TUNA,
SLICED ¼ INCH THICK

1 TABLESPOON CHOPPED FRESH SAGE

1 TABLESPOON CHOPPED FRESH ROSEMARY

2 DRIED BAY LEAVES, CRUMBLED

1 TEASPOON DRIED CHILI FLAKES

SALT AND GROUND BLACK PEPPER

FRESH BAY LEAVES

2 LEMONS, EACH CUT INTO 6 WEDGES

1 TABLESPOON OLIVE OIL

1 TABLESPOON LEMON JUICE

◆ Place tuna slices between sheets of plastic wrap and beat gently with a meat tenderizer or rolling pin until thin.

◆ Mix sage, rosemary, dried bay leaves, and chili flakes together. Sprinkle mixture over tuna slices and season with salt and pepper.

◆ Roll up each slice of tuna neatly. Thread onto skewers, alternately with fresh bay leaves and lemon wedges. Brush with olive oil and lemon juice, mixed together.

◆ Place in the grilling machine and grill 4 to 6 minutes until just cooked. Alternatively, cook on a preheated grill 2 or 3 minutes on each side.

Salmon and Dill Burgers

MAKES 4 SERVINGS

1 POUND SKINLESS, BONELESS SALMON, GROUND

½ CUP MASHED POTATO

¼ CUP CHOPPED FRESH DILL

2 TABLESPOONS CHOPPED DILL PICKLE

1 TEASPOON GREEN PEPPERCORNS IN BRINE, CRUSHED

SALT TO TASTE

SUNFLOWER OIL FOR BRUSHING

4 BAGELS, SPLIT LENGTHWISE

¼ CUP CREAM CHEESE

WATERCRESS SPRIGS

SLICED DILL PICKLES

◆ Place ground salmon, potato, dill, dill pickle, peppercorns, and salt in a bowl and mix well. Divide into 4 and shape into patties. Brush with oil.

◆ Place burgers in the grilling machine and grill 6 to 8 minutes until cooked through. Alternatively, cook on a preheated grill 4 minutes on each side.

◆ To serve, spread 1 tablespoon of cream cheese on the bottom half of each bagel, top with some watercress and a burger. Finish with sliced dill pickles and bagel tops. Serve at once, accompanied by potato salad if desired.

Phuket Crab Cakes

MAKES 4 SERVINGS

2 TABLESPOONS BUTTER

¼ CUP FLOUR

⅔ CUP MILK

1 POUND CRABMEAT, FLAKED

1½ CUPS FRESH WHITE BREADCRUMBS

¼ CUP CHOPPED FRESH CILANTRO

2 TABLESPOONS LIME ZEST

3 TABLESPOONS LIME JUICE

3 TABLESPOONS GRATED FRESH GINGER

4 TEASPOONS SOY SAUCE

1 FRESH RED CHILE, SEEDED AND CHOPPED

VEGETABLE OIL FOR BRUSHING

◆ Melt butter in a saucepan and stir in flour to make a roux. Gradually add milk, whisking well between each addition, and boil 2 or 3 minutes to form a thick white sauce.

◆ Remove sauce from the heat and stir in crab, breadcrumbs, cilantro, lime zest and juice, ginger, soy sauce, chile, and seasoning. Let cool.

◆ When mixture is cool, shape it into 8 cakes. Refrigerate crab cakes at least 2 hours before cooking them.

◆ Brush crab cakes with a little oil, place in the grilling machine, and grill 6 to 8 minutes. Alternatively, cook on a preheated grill 4 minutes on each side.

◆ Serve crab cakes at once, with a salad and chili sauce, if desired.

Mediterranean Grilled Sardines

MAKES 4 TO 6 SERVINGS

12 SMALL SARDINES

12 SMALL STRIPS LEMON PEEL

12 SMALL ROSEMARY SPRIGS

4 TO 6 LEMON WEDGES, TO SERVE

HERB AND LEMON OIL

¼ CUP EXTRA VIRGIN OLIVE OIL

2 TEASPOONS GRATED LEMON ZEST

JUICE 1 LEMON

1 TABLESPOON CHOPPED FRESH ROSEMARY

1 TABLESPOON CHOPPED FRESH THYME

◆ Wash sardines and dry on absorbent kitchen paper. Stuff a strip of lemon peel and a rosemary sprig into each fish. Place in a shallow dish.

◆ To make herb and lemon oil, mix together in a bowl olive oil, lemon zest and juice, rosemary, and thyme. Season with salt and pepper and pour over sardines. Leave in a cool place to marinate 1 hour.

◆ Thread 3 sardines onto each pair of skewers by pushing one skewer through a sardine just below the head and the other in just above the tail.

◆ Place sardines in the grilling machine and grill 6 or 7 minutes. Alternatively, cook on a hot grill 3 or 4 minutes on each side, basting with more oil while cooking.

◆ Serve 2 or 3 sardines to each person, with lemon wedges.

Salmon with Capers and Gazpacho Salsa

MAKES 4 SERVINGS

3 TABLESPOONS OLIVE OIL

GRATED ZEST AND JUICE 1 LIME

1 TABLESPOON CAPERS IN BRINE, DRAINED

4 SALMON STEAKS

GAZPACHO SALSA

4 TOMATOES, PEELED, SEEDED AND DICED

½ LARGE CUCUMBER, DICED

½ ONION, DICED

½ RED BELL PEPPER, DICED

1 TABLESPOON EACH CHOPPED FRESH PARSLEY AND CILANTRO

1 TEASPOON GRANULATED SUGAR

2 TABLESPOONS RED WINE VINEGAR

◆ In a bowl mix together olive oil, lime zest and juice, capers and a pinch of salt. Place salmon steaks in a shallow dish and pour over marinade. Cover and refrigerate salmon 2 hours, if time permits.

◆ To make salsa, put diced tomatoes, cucumber, onion and red bell pepper in a bowl with chopped parsley and cilantro, sugar and wine vinegar. Season to taste with salt and pepper. Cover and refrigerate until required.

◆ Remove salmon steaks from marinade and press a few capers into flesh of each one. Reserve remaining marinade for basting.

◆ Place salmon in the grilling machine and grill 5 or 6 minutes. Alternatively, place on a preheated grill and cook 4 or 5 minutes on each side, basting occasionally with marinade.

◆ Serve salmon hot with gazpacho salsa.

Spanish-style Shrimp

MAKES 4 SERVINGS

*1 POUND LARGE RAW SHRIMP, PEELED BUT
WITH TAILS LEFT ON*

⅓ CUP EXTRA VIRGIN OLIVE OIL

½ GARLIC CLOVE, FINELY CRUSHED

JUICE 1 LEMON

SALT AND GROUND BLACK PEPPER

*1 LARGE TOMATO, PEELED, SEEDED,
AND FINELY CHOPPED*

½ SMALL RED CHILE, SEEDED AND CHOPPED

1 TABLESPOON CHOPPED FRESH PARSLEY

*PARSLEY SPRIGS AND LEMON SLICES
AND ZEST, TO GARNISH*

◆ Using a small sharp knife, make a fine cut along the spine of each shrimp and remove black vein. Place shrimp in a shallow dish.

◆ In a small bowl, stir together 2 tablespoons oil, garlic, 1½ tablespoons lemon juice, salt, and pepper. Pour over shrimp and leave 30 minutes.

◆ Lift shrimp from dish and thread onto skewers. Pace in the grilling machine and grill 3 or 4 minutes until pink. Alternatively, brush with any remaining marinade and cook on a preheated grill 2 or 3 minutes on each side.

◆ In another small bowl, stir together remaining oil and lemon juice, tomato, chile, parsley, and salt and pepper. Spoon over hot shrimp.

◆ Serve shrimp garnished with parsley sprigs and lemon slices and zest.

Poultry

Chicken with Chile and Lime

4 TEASPOONS CHILI OIL

2 TABLESPOONS CLEAR HONEY

¼ CUP CHOPPED FRESH CILANTRO

2 GARLIC CLOVES, CRUSHED

GRATED ZEST AND JUICE 2 LIMES

6 CHICKEN FILLETS

CILANTRO AND CHILE YOGURT

½ CUP PLAIN YOGURT

½ TEASPOON CHILI OIL

GRATED ZEST AND JUICE 1 LIME

¼ CUP CHOPPED FRESH CILANTRO

1 SMALL FRESH RED CHILE, SEEDED AND FINELY CHOPPED

◆ To make marinade, place chili oil, honey, cilantro, garlic, and lime zest and juice in a shallow glass dish and mix well to combine.

◆ With a sharp knife, make several deep slashes in each chicken fillet. Place chicken in dish of marinade and turn to coat well. Cover and refrigerate 3 to 4 hours.

◆ To make cilantro and chile yogurt, in a bowl mix together yogurt, chili oil, lime zest and juice, chopped cilantro, chopped red chile, and a pinch of salt. Cover and refrigerate until required.

◆ Remove chicken from marinade and place in the grilling machine. Grill 10 to 12 minutes. To test if chicken is cooked, pierce thickest part with a skewer. If juices are still pink, cook until juices run clear.

◆ Alternatively, place chicken, skin side up, on a medium-hot grill and cook 10 minutes, brushing occasionally with marinade. Turn chicken fillets over and cook an additional 10 minutes.

◆ Serve at once with cilantro and chile yogurt.

Thai Garlic Chicken

4 CHICKEN FILLETS

4 GARLIC CLOVES, SLICED

1 TABLESPOON FINELY CHOPPED FRESH GINGER

GRATED ZEST AND JUICE 1 LIME

3 TABLESPOONS SUNFLOWER OIL

1 TABLESPOON DARK SOY SAUCE

1 OR 2 FRESH RED CHILES, SEEDED AND THINLY SLICED

2 TABLESPOONS CHOPPED FRESH CILANTRO

◆ Cut 2 or 3 slashes through the skin and flesh of each chicken fillet. Place chicken fillets in a glass dish.

◆ In a bowl, mix together garlic, ginger, lime zest and juice, sunflower oil, soy sauce, chiles, and cilantro.

◆ Pour marinade over chicken, cover, and refrigerate at least 2 hours. Bring to room temperature before cooking.

◆ Lift chicken from marinade, place in the grilling machine, and grill 10 to 12 minutes. Alternatively, cook chicken on a medium-hot grill 8 to 10 minutes on each side, basting occasionally with marinade while cooking.

Cajun Chicken Salad

4 SKINLESS CHICKEN FILLETS

2 TABLESPOONS UNSALTED BUTTER, MELTED

2 CORN ON THE COB, EACH CUT INTO 6 PIECES

2 LARGE RED BELL PEPPERS

3 CUPS COARSELY SHREDDED ICEBERG LETTUCE

OREGANO SPRIGS, TO GARNISH

SEASONING MIX

1½ TEASPOONS SALT

1 TABLESPOON PAPRIKA

1 TEASPOON DRIED ONION GRANULES

1 TEASPOON DRIED GARLIC GRANULES

1 TEASPOON DRIED THYME

1 TEASPOON CAYENNE

½ TEASPOON CRACKED BLACK PEPPER

½ TEASPOON DRIED OREGANO

SPICY DRESSING

⅓ CUP CORN OIL

2 TABLESPOONS LEMON JUICE

1 SHALLOT, FINELY CHOPPED

¼ TEASPOON CAYENNE

1 TEASPOON DIJON-STYLE MUSTARD

1 TEASPOON CHOPPED FRESH THYME

PINCH SUGAR

SALT AND GROUND BLACK PEPPER

◆ To make spicy dressing, place corn oil, lemon juice, shallot, cayenne, mustard, fresh thyme, sugar, and salt and pepper in screw-top jar and shake to combine. Chill until required.

◆ To make seasoning mix, place salt, paprika, dried onion and garlic granules, dried thyme, cayenne, black pepper, and dried oregano in a bowl and stir to combine.

◆ Place each chicken fillet between sheets of plastic wrap and flatten with a meat tenderizer or rolling pin until about ½ inch thick.

◆ Brush each chicken fillet with some melted butter and press one-quarter of seasoning mix over each breast to coat completely. Set aside.

◆ Cook corn in boiling, salted water 20 to 25 minutes until tender.

◆ Meanwhile, cut each bell pepper into quarters lengthwise, core and seed, and brush with a little oil.

◆ Grill bell peppers in the grilling machine 10 minutes. Alternatively, cook on a grill 10 to 15 minutes, turning occasionally until beginning to blacken. Keep warm.

◆ Place chicken in the grilling machine and grill 6 to 8 minutes until the outside is blackened and chicken is cooked through. Alternatively, cook on a preheated grill 5 or 6 on each side.

◆ Toss iceberg lettuce in spicy dressing. Cut red pepper into thick strips. Divide lettuce between 4 plates. Slice chicken fillets and divide between plates. Place 3 pieces of corn and some red pepper strips on each plate. Serve at once.

Moroccan Chicken in Pita

MAKES 4 TO 6 SERVINGS

SCANT ½ CUP PLAIN YOGURT

2 TEASPOONS HARISSA PASTE

2 TEASPOONS GROUND CUMIN

2 TEASPOONS GROUND CORIANDER

2 GARLIC CLOVES, CRUSHED

1 TABLESPOON OLIVE OIL

SALT AND GROUND BLACK PEPPER

4 SKINLESS CHICKEN FILLETS

PITA BREAD, SHREDDED LETTUCE, AND CHOPPED TOMATOES, TO SERVE

◆ In a bowl mix together yogurt, harissa paste, cumin, coriander, garlic, olive oil, salt, and pepper.

◆ Place chicken fillets in a dish and spread over marinade. Cover dish and refrigerate 2 hours.

◆ Remove chicken from marinade and place in the grilling machine. Grill 10 to 12 minutes until browned and juices run clear when chicken is pierced with a knife. Alternatively, cook on a preheated grill 10 minutes on each side.

◆ Meanwhile, place pita in bun warmer 5 minutes to warm through.

◆ To serve, cut chicken into thin slices. Cut pita bread in half and open to form pockets. Fill pockets with sliced chicken, shredded lettuce, and chopped tomatoes.

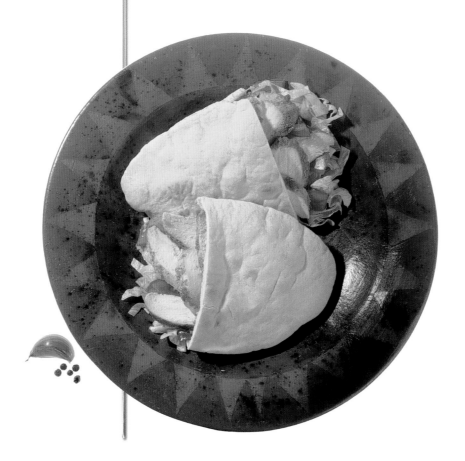

Marinated Chicken Salad

MAKES 4 TO 6 SERVINGS

⅔ CUP OLIVE OIL

¼ CUP BALSAMIC VINEGAR

2 TABLESPOONS CHOPPED FRESH BASIL

2 TABLESPOONS CHOPPED FRESH ROSEMARY

2 GARLIC CLOVES, CRUSHED

4 SKINLESS CHICKEN FILLETS

1 RED BELL PEPPER, SEEDED AND QUARTERED

1 YELLOW BELL PEPPER, SEEDED AND QUARTERED

2 ZUCCHINI, CUT INTO ½-INCH THICK SLICES

2 LARGE OPEN-CUP MUSHROOMS

½ CUP PINE NUTS, TOASTED

8 SUN-DRIED TOMATOES, DRAINED AND CHOPPED

½ TEASPOON SUGAR

SALT AND PEPPER

◆ In a bowl, mix together ¼ cup olive oil, 2 tablespoons vinegar, 1 tablespoon basil, 1 tablespoon rosemary, and the garlic. Place chicken in a shallow, flameproof dish and pour over marinade. Cover and let marinate 30 minutes.

◆ Remove chicken from marinade, place in the grilling machine, and grill 10 to 12 minutes. Alternatively, place chicken on a preheated grill and cook 10 minutes on each side, brushing occasionally with marinade.

◆ Brush bell peppers, zucchini, and mushrooms with 2 tablespoons oil. Place in the grilling machine and grill about 8 to 10 minutes. Cool, then peel skins from peppers and cut mushrooms into quarters. Alternatively, cook on a preheated grill 10 to 14 minutes on each side.

◆ Slice chicken fillets and place in a dish with grilled vegetables. Sprinkle over toasted pine nuts and sun-dried tomatoes.

◆ In a small jug, mix together remaining herbs, oil, and vinegar. Add sugar and season with a little salt and pepper. Pour over chicken and vegetables and marinate 1 hour, stirring occasionally, before serving.

Chicken Pinwheels

3 TABLESPOONS PISTACHIO NUTS

¼ CUP FRESH WHITE BREADCRUMBS

½ STICK BUTTER, MELTED

40 BASIL LEAVES, TORN

SALT AND GROUND BLACK PEPPER

1 SMALL LEEK, CUT INTO 2 LENGTHS

4 SKINLESS CHICKEN FILLETS

2 TABLESPOONS OLIVE OIL FOR BRUSHING

1¼ CUPS LIGHT CREAM

◆ To make stuffing, place pistachio nuts, breadcrumbs, melted butter, 24 torn basil leaves, and salt and pepper in a bowl and mix well.

◆ Blanch leeks 3 minutes, then drain and refresh in cold water. Slice each piece of leek in half lengthwise. Dry on absorbent kitchen paper.

◆ Place each chicken fillet between sheets of plastic wrap and flatten with a meat tenderizer or rolling pin. Spread one-quarter of stuffing onto each fillet, leaving ½-inch border. Place a piece of leek in center and roll up to enclose stuffing. Secure with string. Refrigerate 2 hours.

◆ Brush pinwheels with a little olive oil and grill in the grilling machine 10-15 minutes, turning a half turn and brushing with oil half way through cooking time. Alternatively, cook on a hot grill 20 to 25 minutes, turning and brushing with oil occasionally.

◆ Place cream, remaining basil, and seasoning in a pan and boil rapidly 4 or 5 minutes. Slice pinwheels thickly and serve with sauce.

Chicken Bagna Cauda

4 CHICKEN FILLETS

6 TABLESPOONS CHOPPED FRESH PARSLEY

8 GARLIC CLOVES

1¼ CUPS OLIVE OIL

8 ANCHOVY FILLETS, FINELY CHOPPED

12 HALVES SUN-DRIED TOMATOES IN OIL, DRAINED AND FINELY CHOPPED

2 TABLESPOONS CHILI SAUCE

◆ Make several slashes through skin and flesh of each chicken fillet. Crush 4 garlic cloves and mix together with ¼ cup parsley, ¼ cup olive oil and seasoning. Work into slashes and over surface of each chicken fillet. Place chicken in a shallow dish, pour over any remaining marinade, cover, and refrigerate 2 hours.

◆ To make sauce, heat remaining oil in a saucepan. Crush remaining garlic cloves, add to pan, and sauté 1 minute. Add anchovies, sun-dried tomatoes, chili sauce, remaining 2 tablespoons parsley, and black pepper and simmer gently 3 or 4 minutes. Set sauce aside until required.

◆ Remove chicken from marinade and place in grilling machine. Grill 10-12 minutes. Alternatively cook on a hot grill about 20 minutes, turning and basting occasionally. Test chicken with a skewer: if juices run clear, chicken is cooked. Reheat sauce and serve with cooked chicken.

Spicy Chicken and Corn Burgers

MAKES 4 SERVINGS

2 TABLESPOONS OLIVE OIL

1 ONION, FINELY CHOPPED

2 GARLIC CLOVES, CRUSHED

1 TABLESPOON PAPRIKA

1½ POUNDS GROUND CHICKEN

½ CUP CANNED CORN KERNELS, DRAINED

SALT AND GROUND BLACK PEPPER

4 HAMBURGER ROLLS, SPLIT LENGTHWISE

LITTLE GEM LETTUCE LEAVES, RED BELL PEPPER RINGS, AND MAYONNAISE, TO SERVE

◆ Heat oil in a pan and cook onion and garlic 4 minutes until soft. Stir in paprika and cook an additional 1 minute. Cool mixture slightly.

◆ Combine mixture with ground chicken, corn, and seasoning. Divide into 4 portions and shape into patties.

◆ Brush burgers with a little oil and place in the grilling machine. Grill 6 to 8 minutes until cooked through. Alternatively, cook burgers on a preheated grill 5 minutes on each side.

◆ Meanwhile, place burger rolls in the bun warmer 5 minutes.

◆ To serve, divide lettuce between 4 bottom halves of rolls, top with red bell pepper rings and burgers, spoon over some mayonnaise, and finish with roll tops.

Chicken Burgers with Tarragon and Prosciutto

MAKES 4 SERVINGS

2 TABLESPOONS VEGETABLE OIL

1 RED ONION, FINELY CHOPPED

2 GARLIC CLOVES, CRUSHED

1½ POUNDS GROUND CHICKEN

SALT AND GROUND BLACK PEPPER

4 OUNCES PROSCIUTTO, CUT INTO THIN STRIPS

2 TABLESPOONS CHOPPED FRESH TARRAGON

BUTTER, SOFTENED, FOR SPREADING

4 MIXED-GRAIN ROLLS SPLIT LENGTHWISE

LETTUCE LEAVES, TO SERVE

◆ Heat oil in a pan and cook onion and garlic 3 minutes until soft. Cool mixture and place in a bowl with chicken and seasoning; mix well to combine. Divide into 8 equal portions and shape into patties.

◆ Place one-quarter of prosciutto and tarragon in the center of each of 4 patties. Place other 4 patties over these and reshape to make 4 stuffed burgers.

◆ Brush burgers with a little oil and place in the grilling machine. Grill 6 to 8 minutes until cooked through. Alternatively cook burgers on a pre-heated grill 4½ minutes on each side.

◆ Meanwhile, place rolls in the bun warmer 5 minutes.

◆ To serve, divide lettuce between 4 bottom halves of rolls. Top each with a burger and finish with roll tops. Serve at once.

Cajun Turkey Kabobs

MAKES 4 SERVINGS

1 SMALL ONION, CHOPPED

2 GARLIC CLOVES, CHOPPED

1 TABLESPOON EACH CHOPPED FRESH
OREGANO AND THYME

1½ TEASPOONS PAPRIKA

½ TEASPOON CAYENNE

JUICE ½ LEMON

⅓ CUP CORN OIL

1¼ POUNDS TURKEY FILLET, DICED

8 BABY CORN

8 SHALLOTS, UNPEELED

1 LARGE GREEN BELL PEPPER, CORED,
SEEDED, AND CHOPPED

16 BAY LEAVES

SAFFRON RICE, TO SERVE (OPTIONAL)

◆ Place chopped onion and garlic, fresh oregano and thyme, paprika, cayenne, lemon juice, ¼ cup corn oil, and seasoning in a food processor and blend to a smooth paste.

◆ Pour marinade into a glass bowl and add diced turkey, turning to coat well. Cover and refrigerate 4 hours.

◆ Blanch baby corn 1 minute. Blanch shallots 5 minutes, then peel.

◆ Thread marinated turkey onto skewers, alternating with baby corn, shallots, bell peppers, and bay leaves.

◆ Place kabobs in a grilling machine and grill 7 or 8 minutes. Alternatively, cook kabobs on a prepared, medium-hot grill about 7 minutes on each side, brushing occasionally with remaining marinade.

◆ Serve kabobs at once, with saffron rice if desired.

Tandoori Turkey

MAKES 6 TO 8 SERVINGS

6 SKINLESS TURKEY FILLETS

JUICE 3 SMALL LEMONS

1 CUP PLAIN YOGURT

½ CUP SALAD OIL

4 GARLIC CLOVES, CRUSHED

2 TEASPOONS PAPRIKA

2 TEASPOONS GROUND CUMIN

4 TEASPOONS TURMERIC

½ TEASPOON GROUND GINGER

2 TEASPOONS SALT

◆ Make a few deep slashes in turkey fillets on both sides. Place turkey in a single layer in a large, shallow, non-porous dish.

◆ Mix together lemon juice, yogurt, oil, garlic, paprika, cumin, turmeric, ginger, and salt. Pour over turkey fillets and turn to coat well. Cover and marinate in the refrigerator at least 12 hours.

◆ Remove turkey from marinade and place in the grilling machine. Grill 8 to 10 minutes.

◆ Alternatively, cook turkey fillets on a preheated hot grill 10 minutes on each side, basting frequently with marinade while cooking, until cooked through.

Turkey, Orange and Thyme Burgers

MAKES 4 SERVINGS

1½ POUNDS GROUND TURKEY

1 SHALLOT, FINELY CHOPPED

2 TABLESPOONS CHOPPED FRESH THYME

2 TABLESPOONS GRATED ORANGE ZEST

SALT AND GROUND BLACK PEPPER

8 SLICES SOURDOUGH RYE BREAD

CORN SALAD, TO SERVE

MAYONNAISE, TO SERVE

CRANBERRY RELISH

½ CUP CRANBERRY SAUCE

1 TABLESPOON GOLDEN RAISINS

1 TABLESPOON CHOPPED FRESH THYME

1 ORANGE, SEGMENTED AND
COARSELY CHOPPED

◆ Place turkey, shallot, thyme, orange zest, and salt and pepper in a bowl and mix well to combine. Divide mixture into 4 portions and shape into patties.

◆ To make cranberry relish, place cranberry sauce, sultanas, thyme, and orange pieces in a bowl and toss gently to combine. Chill until required.

◆ Brush burgers with a little oil and place in the grilling machine. Grill 6 to 8 minutes until cooked through. Alternatively, cook burgers on a preheated grill 4 minutes on each side. Keep warm.

◆ Place slices of bread in the grilling machine and grill 2 or 3 minutes until lightly toasted. Alternatively, toast bread on the preheated grill.

◆ To serve, divide corn salad between 4 slices of bread, top with mayonnaise and a burger, and place a spoonful of cranberry relish on each burger. Top burgers with remaining slices of bread and serve at once with extra relish and mayonnaise.

Duck Breast with Port and Cherries

◆ Make several deep slashes through skin and flesh of each duck breast.

◆ In a bowl, mix together rosemary, cinnamon, allspice, soft brown sugar, and vegetable oil. Work this mixture into slashes and surface of duck breasts. Cover and refrigerate at least 2 hours.

◆ To make sauce, place port, vinegar, and sugar in a saucepan and bring to a boil. Boil sauce 4 or 5 minutes to reduce it.

◆ Add cherries, reduce heat, and cook very gently an additional 6 to 8 minutes. Taste and adjust seasoning, if necessary, and set sauce aside until required.

◆ Place duck breasts in the grilling machine and grill 12 to 15 minutes until cooked through. Alternatively, cook on a medium-hot grill about 10 minutes on each side.

◆ Reheat sauce. Slice duck breasts and serve with sauce, accompanied by new potatoes, if desired.

Duck Breasts with Crisp Polenta

2 TABLESPOONS CHOPPED FRESH SAGE

1 TABLESPOON CHOPPED FRESH ROSEMARY

SALT AND GROUND BLACK PEPPER

1 CUP QUICK-COOK POLENTA

1 TABLESPOON OLIVE OIL

2 DUCK BREASTS

PINCH GROUND ALLSPICE

ROSEMARY AND SAGE SPRIGS, TO GARNISH

TOMATO SAUCE

2¼ POUNDS FRESH RIPE TOMATOES, QUARTERED

1 MEDIUM ONION, CHOPPED

2 GARLIC CLOVES, CHOPPED

4 FRESH BASIL LEAVES, BRUISED

3 TABLESPOONS OLIVE OIL

◆ To make tomato sauce, place tomatoes, onion, and garlic in a large saucepan. Cover, bring to a boil, then cook slowly 25 minutes. Uncover saucepan and simmer another 15 to 30 minutes. Purée sauce in a blender, then strain to remove any seeds and skin. Stir in basil and oil.

◆ Bring 2½ cups water to a boil with herbs, salt, and pepper. Sprinkle in polenta, whisking to prevent lumps forming. Turn down heat and simmer polenta 5 to 10 minutes, stirring constantly until very thick.

◆ Turn out polenta onto a wooden board and shape into a loaf. Cool, cover, and chill 1 hour.

◆ Cut polenta into 4 thick slices. Brush with some of the olive oil and place in the grilling machine. Grill 4 to 6 minutes until crisp and golden. Alternatively, place on a preheated grill and cook 4 or 5 minutes on each side until golden. Keep warm.

◆ Rub duck breasts with allspice, then brush with a little olive oil. Place in the grilling machine and grill 10 to 12 minutes. Alternatively, cook on a preheated grill 8 to 10 minutes on each side.

◆ Slice each duck breast into 4 and top each polenta slice with 2 pieces. Garnish with herb sprigs and serve with tomato sauce.

Meat

Italian Burgers

MAKES 4 SERVINGS

¾ CUP OLIVE OIL

1 TABLESPOON SUN-DRIED TOMATO PASTE

2 GARLIC CLOVES, CRUSHED

1 TABLESPOON CHOPPED FRESH THYME

¼ CUP CHOPPED FRESH OREGANO

1½ POUNDS GROUND BEEF

4 OUNCES FULL-FLAVORED ITALIAN SALAMI,
FINELY CHOPPED

SALT AND GROUND BLACK PEPPER

8 OUNCES MOZZARELLA CHEESE,
CUT INTO 4 SLICES

4 PIECES FOCACCIA BREAD

OAK LEAF LETTUCE, SLICED BEEFSTEAK
TOMATOES, AND SLICED RED ONIONS,
TO SERVE

◆ To make marinade, place olive oil, sun-dried tomato paste, crushed garlic, thyme, and 1 teaspoon chopped oregano in a bowl and mix well to combine.

◆ Place beef, salami, remaining oregano, and seasoning in a bowl and mix well to combine. Divide mixture into 4 and shape into patties.

◆ Place patties in a single layer in a glass dish and pour over marinade. Cover and chill at least 2 hours or, preferably, overnight.

◆ Place burgers in the grilling machine and grill 7 or 8 minutes. Top each burger with a slice of Mozzarella and grill 30 seconds.

◆ Alternatively, cook burgers on a preheated grill 5 minutes on each side, basting with reserved marinade while cooking. Top each burger with a slice of Mozzarella and grill an additional 1½ minutes.

◆ Place bread in the bun warmer 4 or 5 minutes. Slice lengthwise.

◆ To serve, divide lettuce and tomato between 4 bottom pieces of bread. Place a burger on each and top with red onion slices. Finish with top slices of bread .

Steaks with Chili Sauce

MAKES 4 SERVINGS

4 LEAN BEEF FILLETS, EACH WEIGHING ABOUT 4 OUNCES

1 TEASPOON DARK SOY SAUCE

1 GARLIC CLOVE, FINELY CHOPPED

1 TEASPOON SESAME OIL

2 TABLESPOONS CHOPPED FRESH CHIVES, TO GARNISH

CHILI SAUCE

1 TEASPOON SUNFLOWER OIL

1 FRESH GREEN CHILE, SEEDED AND FINELY CHOPPED

1 SHALLOT, FINELY CHOPPED

1 TEASPOON CHILI SAUCE

2 TABLESPOONS RED RICE VINEGAR

¼ CUP DRY SHERRY

1 TEASPOON BROWN SUGAR

◆ Trim any fat from steaks. Tenderize lightly with a meat tenderizer or rolling pin.

◆ Mix together soy sauce, garlic, and sesame oil in a small bowl and brush over steaks.

◆ Place steaks in the grilling machine and grill 5 to 7 minutes. Alternatively, cook on a preheated grill 3 or 4 minutes on each side, brushing with soy sauce mixture to prevent drying out.

◆ Meanwhile, make chili sauce. Heat oil in a pan and stir-fry chile and shallot over a low heat 1 minute. Stir in chili sauce, red rice vinegar, sherry, and brown sugar and simmer 2 or 3 minutes.

◆ Drain cooked steaks on absorbent kitchen paper. Sprinkle with chives and serve with sauce, accompanied by a salad if desired.

Beef and Bean Burgers

MAKES 4 SERVINGS

1 POUND GROUND BEEF

1 CUP CANNED RED KIDNEY BEANS,
CHOPPED

1 SMALL ONION, FINELY CHOPPED

2 GARLIC CLOVES, CRUSHED

1 TEASPOON CHILI POWDER

CRISP GREEN LETTUCE LEAVES

4 THICK SLICES AVOCADO

1 RED ONION, SLICED INTO RINGS

¼ CUP CILANTRO LEAVES

4 FLOUR TORTILLAS, WARMED

¼ CUP SOUR CREAM

◆ Place beef, beans, onion, garlic, chili powder, and salt and pepper in a bowl and mix well to combine. Divide mixture into 4 and shape into equal-size patties. Chill until required.

◆ Just before cooking, brush each burger with a little oil. Place in the grilling machine and grill 7 or 8 minutes. Alternatively, preheat a grill and cook burgers about 6 minutes on each side

◆ Meanwhile, place tortillas in the bun warmer 3 or 4 minutes.

◆ Divide lettuce leaves, avocado and red onion slices, and cilantro leaves between tortillas. Top each with a burger and spoon some sour cream on each one to serve.

California Dogs

MAKES 4 SERVINGS

7-OUNCE CAN CORN KERNELS, DRAINED

¼ GREEN BELL PEPPER, FINELY DICED

4 RADISHES, FINELY SLICED

½ RED ONION, FINELY DICED

1 GARLIC CLOVE, CRUSHED

JUICE ½ LEMON

1 TABLESPOON CHOPPED FRESH PARSLEY

4 LARGE FRANKFURTERS

4 PLAIN OR GRANARY HOT DOG ROLLS

BUTTER, SOFTENED, FOR SPREADING

6 SMALL LETTUCE LEAVES, TOMATO SLICES,
AND ONION RINGS, TO SERVE

◆ Place corn kernels, green bell pepper, radishes, red onion, garlic, lemon juice, and parsley in a bowl and season to taste with salt and pepper. Cover and refrigerate.

◆ Make several diagonal slashes in each frankfurter. Place in the grilling machine and grill 5 or 6 minutes. Alternatively cook on a preheated grill 4 minutes on each side.

◆ Meanwhile, place hot dog rolls in the bun warmer 3 or 4 minutes. Spread a little softened butter in rolls.

◆ Tear lettuce leaves into bite-size pieces and divide between 4 rolls. Top each with tomato slices and onion rings, then with a frankfurter.

◆ Serve California dogs at once with the corn salsa.

Steaks with Tomato and Olives

4 FILLET STEAKS, EACH WEIGHING
ABOUT 4 OUNCES

OLIVE OIL FOR BRUSHING

BASIL LEAVES, TO GARNISH

ROASTED SLICED POTATOES AND COOKED
BROCCOLI, TO SERVE (OPTIONAL)

TOMATO AND OLIVE SAUCE

2 TABLESPOONS OLIVE OIL

2 GARLIC CLOVES, CHOPPED

1 MEDIUM ONION, THINLY SLICED

1 CARROT, FINELY DICED

14-OUNCE CAN CHOPPED TOMATOES

1 TEASPOON BALSAMIC VINEGAR

$\frac{1}{2}$ TEASPOON DRIED OREGANO

1 TABLESPOON CHOPPED FRESH BASIL

SALT AND GROUND BLACK PEPPER

12 BLACK OLIVES, PITTED

◆ Lightly brush both sides of steaks with a little olive oil. Set aside.

◆ To make sauce, heat oil in a saucepan and add garlic. Cook gently until golden. Add onion, carrot, and 2 tablespoons water. Cover pan and cook gently 10 minutes until onions are soft, stirring once.

◆ Stir in tomatoes, vinegar, oregano, basil, and seasoning, then simmer, uncovered, 15 minutes, until thick and reduced. Stir in olives and keep warm.

◆ Place steaks in the grilling machine and grill 4 or 5 minutes. Alternatively, heat a ridged griddle on a grill until smoking and cook steaks 2 minutes on each side.

Remove steaks to 4 warm plates and season with salt and pepper. Serve with tomato and olive sauce, garnished with basil leaves. Serve with roasted sliced potatoes and broccoli, if desired.

Rio Grande Burgers

MAKES 4 SERVINGS

1½ POUNDS COARSE-GROUND BEEF

1 SMALL ONION, FINELY CHOPPED

SALT AND GROUND BLACK PEPPER

½ TEASPOON GROUND CUMIN

½ TEASPOON GROUND CORIANDER

2 GARLIC CLOVES, CRUSHED

BUTTER, SOFTENED, FOR SPREADING

4 GRANARY ROLLS, HALVED LENGTHWISE

1 LARGE JALAPEÑO CHILE, THINLY SLICED

LETTUCE LEAVES

1 ONION, SLICED INTO RINGS

SWEET PEPPER MAYONNAISE

⅔ CUP MAYONNAISE

3 TABLESPOONS DICED MIXED-
COLORED BELL PEPPERS

1-2 TABLESPOONS CHOPPED FRESH
CILANTRO

◆ To make sweet pepper mayonnaise, mix together mayonnaise, diced bell peppers, and chopped cilantro in a small bowl. Cover and chill.

◆ Place beef, onion, salt, pepper, cumin, coriander, and garlic in a bowl and mix well. Divide mixture into 4 and shape into patties.

◆ Place burgers in the grilling machine and grill 7 or 8 minutes. Meanwhile, place rolls in the bun warmer.

◆ Alternatively, cook burgers on a preheated grill 4 minutes on each side. Toward the end of the cooking time, butter cut sides of rolls and toast on the grill.

◆ To serve, divide sliced chile, lettuce leaves, and onion rings between 4 bottom halves of rolls. Place a burger on each and top with a spoonful of sweet pepper mayonnaise. Replace roll tops and serve at once.

Beef and Vegetable Kabobs

MAKES 6 SERVINGS

12 BABY ONIONS

24 BUTTON MUSHROOMS

2 RED BELL PEPPERS

2 YELLOW BELL PEPPERS

4 LARGE ZUCCHINI

2 POUNDS LEAN BEEF, DICED

24 BAY LEAVES

MARINADE

⅔ CUP OLIVE OIL

1 TABLESPOON LEMON JUICE

1 TABLESPOON CORIANDER SEEDS, CRUSHED

2 TEASPOONS CUMIN SEEDS, CRUSHED

2 SPRIGS THYME, BRUISED

2 SPRIGS SAGE, BRUISED

1 TEASPOON FRESH GREEN PEPPERCORNS, CRUSHED

PINCH FRESHLY GRATED NUTMEG

HERBY YOGURT SAUCE

1¼ CUPS PLAIN YOGURT

1 TABLESPOON LEMON JUICE

1 TABLESPOON CHOPPED FRESH MINT

1 TABLESPOON CHOPPED FRESH DILL

1 TEASPOON GROUND CUMIN

PINCH CAYENNE

SALT AND PEPPER

◆ Prepare vegetables: peel and halve onions and wash and dry mushrooms. Seed peppers and cut each into 12 pieces. Wash and dry zucchini and cut each into 6 slices.

◆ To make marinade, in a small bowl blend oil and lemon juice together. Add crushed coriander and cumin seeds, bruised thyme and sage, crushed green peppercorns, nutmeg, and salt and pepper.

◆ Place vegetables and beef in a large bowl. Pour over marinade, toss well together, cover, and let marinate several hours or overnight.

◆ To make sauce, in a small bowl mix together yogurt, lemon juice, mint, dill, cumin, and cayenne. Season to taste with salt and pepper and refrigerate until required.

◆ Soak bay leaves in cold water 30 minutes before assembling kabobs. Drain and pat dry with absorbent kitchen paper.

◆ Thread beef, vegetables, and bay leaves alternately onto 12 skewers, place in the grilling machine, and grill 8 to 10 minutes. Beef and vegetables should be browned and tender.

◆ Alternatively, cook kabobs on a preheated grill 15 minutes, turning and basting frequently with any marinade or extra olive oil.

◆ Serve 2 kabobs to each person with a generous spoonful of herby yogurt sauce.

Pork with Herb Sauce

MAKES 4 SERVINGS

¼ cup fresh white breadcrumbs

2 tablespoons white wine vinegar

2 garlic cloves

2 canned anchovy fillets, drained

¼ cup chopped fresh parsley

2 teaspoons capers

1 hard-boiled egg yolk

1 cup extra virgin olive oil

Salt and ground black pepper

4 pork loin chops, about 1 inch thick

◆ In a small bowl, soak breadcrumbs in white wine vinegar.

◆ Meanwhile, using a mortar and pestle, crush garlic with anchovy fillets, parsley, capers, and egg yolk.

◆ Squeeze vinegar from breadcrumbs, then add breadcrumbs to mixture in mortar. Stir in oil in a slow trickle to make a creamy sauce. Add black pepper, and salt if necessary. Set aside.

◆ Place chops in the grilling machine and grill 10 to 12 minutes until lightly browned on both sides and cooked through but still juicy in center. Alternatively, cook on a preheated grill 12 minutes on each side.

◆ Season chops with salt and pepper and spoon over some of the sauce. Serve remaining sauce separately.

Chinese-style Pork

MAKES 4 TO 6 SERVINGS

⅔ CUP BROWN SUGAR

1 TABLESPOON DARK SOY SAUCE

1 TABLESPOON OYSTER SAUCE

2 TABLESPOONS RICE WINE OR DRY SHERRY

1 TEASPOON SESAME OIL

½ TEASPOON SEA SALT

½ TEASPOON EDIBLE RED FOOD COLORING (OPTIONAL)

1½ POUNDS PORK LOIN, CUT INTO LONG STRIPS

SHREDDED CHINESE CABBAGE, TO SERVE

◆ In a small bowl stir together sugar and 3 tablespoons boiling water. until sugar dissolves. Stir in soy sauce, oyster sauce, rice wine or sherry, sesame oil, salt, and red food coloring (if using). Let cool.

◆ Place pork in a medium-size bowl and pour over marinade, turning pork to coat evenly. Let marinate 8 hours or overnight, turning pork in marinade occasionally.

◆ Lift pork from marinade, allowing excess to drain off. Thread meat onto skewers and place in the grilling machine about 7 or 8 minutes, until crisp and cooked.

◆ Alternatively, cook on a preheated grill about 8 minutes, basting several times with reserved marinade.

◆ To serve, remove pork from skewers, cut into bite-size pieces, and serve on a bed of shredded Chinese cabbage.

Chinese Burgers

MAKES 4 SERVINGS

1½ POUNDS GROUND PORK

3 GREEN ONIONS, FINELY CHOPPED

1 TABLESPOON GRATED FRESH GINGER

2 TABLESPOONS SOY SAUCE

16 WATER CHESTNUTS, FINELY CHOPPED

8 CHINESE PANCAKES (AVAILABLE FROM ORIENTAL STORES)

CHILI SAUCE, TO SERVE

CHINESE MARINADE

1 TABLESPOON SESAME OIL

3 TABLESPOONS SUNFLOWER OIL

¼ CUP SOY SAUCE

2 TABLESPOONS CLEAR HONEY

2 TEASPOONS CHINESE FIVE-SPICE POWDER

2 GARLIC CLOVES, CRUSHED

1 STALK FRESH LEMON GRASS, FINELY CHOPPED

BEANSPROUT SALAD

5 OUNCES BEANSPROUTS

6 RADISHES, SLICED

2 OUNCES CUCUMBER, CUT INTO THIN STRIPS

1 GREEN CHILE, SEEDED AND SLICED

3 TABLESPOONS CHOPPED FRESH CILANTRO

◆ Place pork, green onions, ginger, soy sauce, and water chestnuts in a bowl and stir well to combine. Divide mixture into 4 equal portions and shape into burgers. Place in a single layer in a glass dish.

◆ To make marinade, in a bowl mix together sesame and sunflower oils, soy sauce, honey, five-spice powder, garlic, and lemon grass.

◆ Pour marinade over burgers, cover dish, and chill at least 2 hours, or, preferably, overnight.

◆ Place burgers in the grilling machine and grill 7 or 8 minutes. Alternatively, cook on a preheated grill 5 or 6 minutes on each side, basting with reserved marinade during cooking.

◆ To make beansprout salad, combine beansprouts, radishes, cucumber, chile, and cilantro in a bowl and toss well. Meanwhile, place pancakes in the bun warmer 3 or 4 minutes.

◆ Place some salad on 2 pancakes, top with a burger, and fold pancakes over. Repeat with remaining burgers. Serve with chili sauce.

Santiago Burgers

MAKES 4 SERVINGS

1 POUND GROUND PORK

4 OUNCES SPICY CHORIZO SAUSAGE, FINELY CHOPPED

1 CUP COOKED CHICKPEAS, MASHED

½ SMALL GREEN BELL PEPPER, FINELY CHOPPED

SALT AND GROUND BLACK PEPPER

8 SLICES SPANISH COUNTRY BREAD

OLIVE OIL FOR BRUSHING

LETTUCE LEAVES

ONION RINGS AND BLACK OLIVES, TO SERVE

◆ Place pork, chorizo, chickpeas, green bell pepper, and seasoning in a bowl and stir well to combine. Divide mixture into 4 portions and shape into burgers.

◆ Brush burgers with a little vegetable oil and place in the grilling machine. Grill 7 or 8 minutes until cooked through.

◆ Alternatively, cook burgers on a preheated grill 5 minutes on each side. Keep warm.

◆ Brush cut bread slices with olive oil and place in the grilling machine. Grill 3 or 4 minutes. Alternatively, toast lightly on the preheated grill.

◆ To serve, divide lettuce leaves between 4 slices of bread, top each with a burger and a slice of bread.

◆ Serve at once, accompanied by onion rings and black olives.

Spicy Pork Kabobs

MAKES 4 SERVINGS

2 TEASPOONS PAPRIKA

1 TEASPOON FINELY CRUSHED CORIANDER SEEDS

1½ TEASPOONS GROUND CUMIN

1 TEASPOON FINELY CHOPPED FRESH OREGANO

¼ TEASPOON GROUND GINGER

LARGE PINCH GROUND CINNAMON

LARGE PINCH CAYENNE

LARGE PINCH GRATED NUTMEG

1 BAY LEAF, FINELY CRUMBLED

2 TABLESPOONS OLIVE OIL

SALT AND GROUND BLACK PEPPER

1 POUND BONED PORK LOIN, CUT INTO 1-INCH CUBES

LEMON SLICES AND BAY LEAVES, TO SERVE

◆ In a bowl, mix together paprika, coriander, cumin, oregano, ginger, cinnamon, cayenne, nutmeg, bay leaf, olive oil, salt, and pepper.

◆ Add pork and stir to coat evenly with marinade. Cover bowl and leave in the refrigerator 8 to 12 hours, turning pork occasionally in marinade.

◆ Thread pork onto skewers. Place in the grilling machine and grill 7 or 8 minutes, until pork is cooked through but still juicy. Alternatively, cook on a preheated grill about 7 minutes, turning occasionally.

◆ Garnish with lemon slices and bay leaves and serve hot.

Pork Brochettes with Citrus Salsa

MAKES 4 SERVINGS

¼ CUP DRY SHERRY OR RICE WINE

¼ CUP GROUND CORIANDER

¼ CUP SUNFLOWER OIL

4 GARLIC CLOVES, FINELY CHOPPED

6 KAFFIR LIME LEAVES, FINELY CHOPPED

SALT AND GROUND BLACK PEPPER

1 POUND PORK TENDERLOIN, CUT INTO
1½-INCH CUBES

2 SMALL YELLOW BELL PEPPERS, CORED,
SEEDED, AND CHOPPED

8 SMALL ONIONS, HALVED

16 BAY LEAVES

CITRUS SALSA

2 ORANGES

2 PINK GRAPEFRUIT

2 TEASPOONS CHOPPED FRESH THYME

4 TEASPOONS SNIPPED FRESH CHIVES

4 KAFFIR LIME LEAVES, VERY FINELY CHOPPED

SALT AND GROUND BLACK PEPPER

◆ In a bowl, mix together sherry or rice wine, ground coriander, oil, garlic, lime leaves, salt, and pepper. Add diced pork and mix to coat evenly. Cover and refrigerate 4 hours.

◆ Thread pork onto 8 skewers, alternating with bell peppers, onions, and bay leaves. Reserve marinade for basting if cooking on an indoor grill.

◆ To make salsa, peel oranges and grapefruit and cut in between membranes to produce segments. Chop segments roughly. Place in a bowl with thyme, chives, lime leaves, and salt and pepper and toss gently to combine.

◆ Place brochettes in the grilling machine and grill 8 to 10 minutes. Alternatively, cook brochettes on a prepared medium-hot grill about 15 minutes, turning frequently and brushing with marinade.

◆ Serve 2 brochettes to each person, accompanied by citrus salsa.

Lamb and Bacon Brochettes with Red Onion

MAKES 4 SERVINGS

16 SLICES BACON

1 POUND LEAN LAMB, CUT INTO FAIRLY LARGE CHUNKS

¼ CUP CHOPPED FRESH SAGE

¼ CUP OLIVE OIL

SEA SALT AND GROUND BLACK PEPPER

4 SMALL RED ONIONS, UNPEELED AND HALVED

SALAD AND POTATOES, TO SERVE (OPTIONAL)

◆ Remove rind from bacon slices and roll up each slice. Thread lamb chunks and two bacon rolls onto each of 8 skewers.

◆ Mix together sage and oil and season with salt and pepper. Brush oil all over prepared brochettes and onion halves.

◆ Grill onion halves in grilling machine 10 to 12 minutes. Alternatively, cook on a hot grill 8 minutes on each side, brushing with sage oil.

◆ Place lamb and bacon brochettes in the grilling machine and grill 6 to 8 minutes. Alternatively cook on a hot grill 4 or 5 minutes on each side, brushing frequently with sage oil.

◆ Serve 2 lamb and bacon brochettes with 2 grilled red onion halves to each person, accompanied by salad and potatoes, if desired.

Lamb Chops with Garlic, Lemon and Oregano

MAKES 4 SERVINGS

2 GARLIC CLOVES

SEA SALT

4 TEASPOONS CHOPPED FRESH OREGANO

GRATED ZEST AND JUICE 2 SMALL LEMONS

¼ CUP SUNFLOWER OIL

SEA SALT AND GROUND BLACK PEPPER

8 LAMB CHOPS

◆ Using a mortar and pestle, crush garlic to a paste with a little sea salt. Add oregano, lemon zest and juice, oil, and seasoning. Stir well to combine thoroughly.

◆ Place lamb chops in a shallow bowl and pour over marinade. Cover and refrigerate 2 hours, if time permits.

◆ Remove chops from marinade and reserve marinade. Place chops in the grilling machine and grill 4 to 6 minutes. Alternatively, cook on a preheated grill 5 minutes on each side.

◆ Just before serving, heat reserved garlic mixture in a small saucepan and pour it over chops.

Bombay Burgers

2 TABLESPOONS VEGETABLE OIL

1 ONION, FINELY CHOPPED

2 TABLESPOONS CURRY POWDER

1½ TEASPOONS TURMERIC

1½ POUNDS GROUND LAMB

*3 TABLESPOONS COOKED
GREEN PEAS*

SALT AND GROUND BLACK PEPPER

½ CUP PLAIN YOGURT

2 TEASPOONS GARAM MASALA

1 TEASPOON GROUND CUMIN

½ TEASPOON CHILI POWDER

*3 TABLESPOONS CHOPPED
FRESH MINT*

*4 MINI NAAN BREADS,
SPLIT LENGTHWISE*

SMALL LETTUCE LEAVES

PLAIN YOGURT, TO SERVE

TROPICAL MANGO SALSA

*1 SMALL MANGO, PEELED
AND FINELY CHOPPED*

*½ CUP SEEDLESS BLACK GRAPES,
ROUGHLY CHOPPED*

*2 SLICES FRESH PINEAPPLE,
FINELY DICED*

PULP 1 PASSION FRUIT

*1 FRESH GREEN CHILE,
SEEDED AND SLICED*

GRATED ZEST AND JUICE 1 LIME

◆ To make salsa, place chopped mango, grapes, and pineapple, passion fruit pulp, green chile, and lime zest and juice in a bowl. Toss gently to combine and chill 2 to 3 hours to allow flavors to develop.

◆ Heat oil in a pan and cook onions, curry powder, and 1 teaspoon turmeric 3 or 4 minutes until soft. Let cool.

◆ Add ground lamb, peas, and seasoning to curried onion mixture and stir well to combine. Divide mixture into 4 equal portions and shape into patties. Place patties in single layer in a glass dish.

◆ To make marinade, place yogurt, garam masala, ground cumin, chili powder, mint, and remaining ½ teaspoon turmeric in a bowl. Stir well to combine. Pour marinade over patties, cover, and chill at least 2 hours.

◆ Place burgers in the grilling machine and grill 8 to 10 minutes until cooked through. Warm naan breads in the bun warmer 3 or 4 minutes. Alternatively, cook burgers on a preheated grill 7 minutes on each side. Warm naan breads on the grill.

◆ To serve, divide lettuce leaves between 4 bottom halves of naan. Place a spoonful of yogurt over each and top with a burger. Spoon over mango salsa and finish with naan tops. Serve with extra salsa and yogurt.

Souvlakia

MAKES 6 SERVINGS

2 GARLIC CLOVES, CRUSHED

¼ CUP LEMON JUICE

2 TABLESPOONS OLIVE OIL

¼ CUP CHOPPED FRESH OREGANO

SALT AND PEPPER

1 POUND LEAN LAMB

6 BAY LEAVES

OREGANO SPRIGS, TO GARNISH

RED BELL PEPPER SAUCE

3 TEASPOONS OLIVE OIL

1 SMALL ONION, CHOPPED

2 RED BELL PEPPERS, SEEDED AND CHOPPED

1 CUP CHICKEN STOCK

◆ In a bowl, mix together garlic, lemon juice, olive oil, oregano, salt, and pepper. Cut lamb in to ¾-inch cubes. Put lamb into marinade, stir well to coat, and leave in a cool place 2 hours.

◆ To make sauce, heat oil in a saucepan, add onion, and cook until soft. Add red bell peppers and cook over low heat 5 minutes.

◆ Pour in stock and simmer 10 minutes, then push through a strainer or purée in a blender or food processor.

◆ Thread lamb onto skewers, adding bay leaves at intervals. Place in the grilling machine and grill 7 or 8 minutes, or until lamb is brown and crisp on the outside and pink and juicy inside.

◆ Alternatively, cook lamb skewers on a preheated grill, turning from time to time, 10 minutes

◆ Garnish with oregano and serve with sauce.

Lamb Tikka

2¼ POUNDS BONELESS LEG OF LAMB

1 TEASPOON GROUND CUMIN

¾ TEASPOON TURMERIC

SALT

⅓ CUP PLAIN YOGURT

½ SMALL ONION, FINELY CHOPPED

2-INCH PIECE FRESH GINGER, GRATED

2 GARLIC CLOVES, CRUSHED

FEW DROPS RED FOOD COLORING
(OPTIONAL)

1 TEASPOON GARAM MASALA

◆ Trim fat from lamb and cut lamb into 1½-inch cubes.

◆ In a large bowl, stir together cumin, turmeric, salt, yogurt, onion, ginger, and garlic. Add food coloring, if desired.

◆ Add lamb to bowl of marinade and stir to coat thoroughly. Cover and leave in refrigerator 4 to 6 hours to marinate.

◆ Drain lamb from marinade and thread onto 8 short skewers, pressing cubes closely together. Reserve marinade if cooking on a grill.

◆ Place kabobs in the grilling machine and grill 10 to 12 minutes until well browned.

◆ Alternatively, cook kabobs on a preheated grill 15 to 20 minutes, basting with remaining marinade and turning occasionally during cooking

◆ Sprinkle with garam masala and serve at once.

Minted Lamb Cutlets

MAKES 6 SERVINGS

12 LAMB CUTLETS

SALT AND PEPPER

⅓ CUP OLIVE OIL

⅓ CUP DRY WHITE WINE

¼ CUP CHOPPED FRESH MINT

MINT LEAVES, TO GARNISH

RELISH

1 LARGE ONION, VERY FINELY CHOPPED

2 TABLESPOONS WHITE WINE VINEGAR

1 TABLESPOON SUGAR

SALT AND PEPPER

◆ Wash cutlets, pat dry with absorbent kitchen paper, and season with salt and pepper. Place in a large shallow dish.

◆ In a small bowl, blend together olive oil, white wine, and chopped mint. Pour over cutlets, cover, and marinate in the refrigerator several hours, turning occasionally.

◆ Remove cutlets from marinade, reserving marinade.

◆ To make relish, put onion, vinegar, and sugar into a heavy-bottomed saucepan, add reserved marinade, and simmer over a medium heat 10 minutes. Let cool.

◆ Place cutlets in the grilling machine and grill 5 to 7 minutes. Alternatively, cook on a hot grill 4 or 5 minutes on each side.

◆ Serve cutlets hot or cold with relish, garnished with mint leaves.

Lamb and Apricot Skewers

3 TABLESPOONS APRICOT JAM

2 TABLESPOONS SOY SAUCE

¼ CUP VEGETABLE OIL

2 TABLESPOONS CIDER VINEGAR

¾ TEASPOON CAYENNE

2 LARGE GARLIC CLOVES, CRUSHED

GROUND BLACK PEPPER

1¼ POUNDS LAMB FILLET, CUT INTO 24 PIECES

4 SHALLOTS

4 FIRM, RIPE APRICOTS, HALVED

16 BAY LEAVES

◆ In a shallow glass dish, mix together apricot jam, soy sauce, oil, vinegar, cayenne, garlic, and black pepper.

◆ Add lamb pieces to marinade and toss to coat evenly. Cover and refrigerate 2 hours.

◆ Blanch shallots in boiling water 4 minutes. Peel and halve them.

◆ Remove lamb from marinade, reserving marinade for basting if cooking on a grill. Thread 3 chunks of meat, a shallot half, an apricot half, and 2 bay leaves onto each skewer.

◆ Place lamb skewers in the grilling machine and grill 8 to 10 minutes. Alternatively, cook on a preheated grill about 15 minutes, turning and basting with reserved marinade while cooking.

Venison Burgers with Spiced Apples

1 POUND GROUND VENISON

1 TABLESPOON CHOPPED FRESH THYME

1 TABLESPOON CHOPPED FRESH PARSLEY

SALT AND GROUND BLACK PEPPER

8 SLICES BACON

2 LARGE RED-SKINNED APPLES

½ STICK BUTTER

½ TEASPOON GROUND CINNAMON

LARGE PINCH GRATED NUTMEG

4 HAMBURGER ROLLS, SPLIT LENGTHWISE

SOFT LETTUCE LEAVES

◆ Place venison, thyme, parsley, and seasoning in a bowl and stir well to combine. Divide mixture into 4 portions and shape into patties. Wrap 2 slices of bacon around each burger and secure with toothpicks.

◆ Brush burgers with a little oil and place in the grilling machine. Grill 8 to 10 minutes. Meanwhile, place rolls in bun warmer 3 or 4 minutes. Alternatively, cook burgers on a preheated grill 6 minutes on each side until cooked through. Toast cut sides of rolls lightly on the grill.

◆ Meanwhile, prepare spiced apples. Core apples and slice into thick rings. Heat half the butter in a large pan and cook half the apple slices 4 or 5 minutes until tender. Sprinkle over half the cinnamon and nutmeg and keep apples warm while cooking second batch in remaining butter.

◆ To serve, place some soft lettuce on bottom halves of rolls, top with some apple slices and a burger, and finish with roll tops. Serve at once with spiced apples.

Blueberry Venison

MAKES 6 SERVINGS

6 VENISON STEAKS

GRATED ZEST AND JUICE 2 ORANGES

JUICE 1 LEMON

3 TABLESPOONS WHISKEY

½ CUP OLIVE OIL

1 TEASPOON ROSEMARY LEAVES

3 BAY LEAVES, CRUMBLED

1 TEASPOON CELERY SALT

1½ CUPS BLUEBERRIES, STALKS REMOVED

¾ CUP SOFT BROWN SUGAR

1 TABLESPOON LEMON JUICE

ORANGE SLICES, BLUEBERRIES, AND BAY LEAVES, TO GARNISH (OPTIONAL)

◆ Trim venison steaks and place on a chopping board. Flatten with a meat tenderizer or rolling pin.

◆ Mix together orange zest and juice, lemon juice, whiskey, oil, rosemary, bay leaves, and celery salt in a large shallow dish.

◆ Place venison steaks in marinade, turning over to coat both sides. Let marinate in refrigerator 6 to 8 hours, basting occasionally.

◆ In a heavy-bottomed saucepan combine sugar, 1 tablespoon lemon juice, and ⅓ cup water. Heat gently, stirring until sugar dissolves.

◆ Add blueberries and bring to a boil. Reduce heat and cook until pulpy. Keep warm.

◆ Remove venison steaks from marinade and place in the grilling machine. Grill 8 to 10 minutes until tender. Alternatively, cook on a preheated grill 5 to 7 minutes on each side

◆ Garnish venison steaks with orange slices, blueberries, and bay leaves, if desired. Serve with blueberry sauce.

Vegetarian Dishes

Falafel Patties with Yogurt and Mint Dip

MAKES 4 SERVINGS

2 TABLESPOONS VEGETABLE OIL

1 TEASPOON CUMIN SEEDS

1 ONION, FINELY CHOPPED

2 GARLIC CLOVES, CRUSHED

*1 TEASPOON CHOPPED
FRESH GREEN CHILE*

½ TEASPOON TURMERIC

15-OUNCE CAN CHICKPEAS, DRAINED

SALT AND GROUND BLACK PEPPER

½ CUP FRESH WHITE BREADCRUMBS

1 EGG, BEATEN

*2 TABLESPOONS CHOPPED
FRESH CILANTRO*

FLOUR FOR COATING

OIL FOR BRUSHING

LEMON WEDGES, TO SERVE

PITA BREAD, TO SERVE

YOGURT AND MINT DIP

½ CUP PLAIN YOGURT

¼ CUP CHOPPED FRESH MINT

1 TEASPOON LEMON JUICE

PINCH GROUND CUMIN

SALT AND GROUND BLACK PEPPER

◆ To make dip, in a bowl, mix together yogurt, mint, lemon juice, cumin, and seasoning. Cover and refrigerate until required.

◆ Heat vegetable oil in a skillet, add cumin seeds, onion, and garlic and sauté 5 minutes. Add chopped chile and turmeric and cook an additional 2 minutes.

◆ Transfer spice mixture to a blender or food processor, add chickpeas and seasoning, and blend or process briefly until chickpeas are roughly mashed and combined with spices.

◆ Transfer to a bowl and add breadcrumbs, beaten egg, and cilantro. Mix to combine and divide into 8 portions. With floured hands, shape into patties and refrigerate these falafel about 4 hours.

◆ Brush falafel all over with oil. Place in the grilling machine and cook 8 to 10 minutes. Alternatively, place on an oiled griddle plate and cook on a preheated grill 6 or 7 minutes on each side.

◆ Serve hot with dip, lemon wedges, and pita bread.

Eggplant Stacks

MAKES 6 SERVINGS

⅓ CUP OLIVE OIL

1 ONION, FINELY CHOPPED

1 GARLIC CLOVE, CRUSHED

1 RED BELL PEPPER, SEEDED AND CHOPPED

14-OUNCE CAN CHOPPED TOMATOES

¼ CUP SUN-DRIED TOMATOES IN OIL, DRAINED AND CHOPPED

1 TABLESPOON RAISINS

½ TEASPOON SUGAR

2 TEASPOONS BALSAMIC VINEGAR

SALT AND GROUND BLACK PEPPER

1 TEASPOON DRIED MINT

4 MEDIUM LONG-SHAPED EGGPLANTS

FRESH MINT SPRIGS, TO GARNISH

◆ In a saucepan, heat 2 tablespoons olive oil. Add onion and garlic and cook 10 minutes, or until soft.

◆ Add chopped red bell pepper, canned tomatoes, sun-dried tomatoes, raisins, sugar, vinegar, salt, pepper, and mint. Simmer gently, uncovered, 20 minutes, or until mixture has thickened.

◆ Meanwhile, cut eggplants into ¼-½-inch thick slices. Brush each slice on both sides with remaining olive oil.

◆ Place eggplant slices in the grilling machine and grill 8 to 10 minutes until soft and browned. Alternatively, heat a ridged cast-iron griddle and cook on a preheated grill 3 or 4 minutes on each side. Keep hot while cooking remaining slices.

◆ Spoon a little of the tomato mixture on an eggplant slice. Top with a second slice of eggplant. Keep warm. Repeat with remaining eggplant slices and tomato mixture.

◆ Serve eggplant stacks hot, garnished with mint sprigs.

Broccoli Pancake Rolls

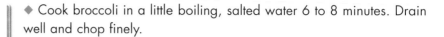

MAKES 6 TO 8 SERVINGS

8 OUNCES BROCCOLI SPEARS

⅓ CUP PLAIN YOGURT

BLACK PEPPER

2 TABLESPOONS ALL-PURPOSE FLOUR

3 TABLESPOONS MILK

4 EGGS

1 TABLESPOON SOY SAUCE

BUTTER

VEGETABLE OIL FOR BRUSHING

◆ Cook broccoli in a little boiling, salted water 6 to 8 minutes. Drain well and chop finely.

◆ Mix broccoli with yogurt and season well with black pepper. Cover and set aside.

◆ Sift flour into a mixing bowl and blend in milk. Beat eggs and soy sauce together and add gradually to flour mixture, beating well to form a smooth thin batter. Pour into a jug.

◆ Heat a small skillet, add a small piece of butter and make 6 to 8 thin (6-inch) omelet-style pancakes, browning them on one side only. (If necessary, grease skillet with a little butter after making each pancake.)

◆ Remove pancakes carefully (they set as they cool) and spread out, cooked sides up, on nonstick baking parchment.

◆ Spoon a little broccoli filling on one edge of the browned side of each pancake. Fold over to enclose filling, tucking in sides, and fold again to form a package.

◆ Brush cool pancakes rolls with oil. Place in the grilling machine and cook 4 or 5 minutes until crisp. Alternatively, place rolls, seam sides down, on a preheated grill and cook 3 or 4 minutes, then turn them over and cook an additional 3 or 4 minutes.

Artichokes with Red Bell Pepper Sauce

MAKES 3 OR 4 SERVINGS

⅓ CUP OLIVE OIL

1 GARLIC CLOVE, CRUSHED

2 TABLESPOONS CHOPPED FRESH PARSLEY

SALT AND GROUND BLACK PEPPER

6 BABY ARTICHOKES

FLAT-LEAF PARSLEY SPRIGS, TO GARNISH

RED BELL PEPPER SAUCE

1 TABLESPOON OLIVE OIL

1 SMALL ONION, CHOPPED

2 RED BELL PEPPERS, DICED

1 CUP VEGETABLE STOCK

◆ In a small bowl, mix together olive oil, garlic, parsley, and salt and pepper. Set aside.

◆ To make red bell pepper sauce, heat oil in a saucepan, add onion and cook 5 minutes until soft.

◆ Add red bell peppers and cook over a low heat 5 minutes, then pour in stock, bring to a boil, and simmer 10 minutes.

◆ Push peppers through a strainer or purée in a food processor or blender. Season with salt and ground black pepper to taste.

◆ Trim bases of artichokes and remove any tough outer leaves. Cut artichokes in half lengthwise and immediately brush with seasoned oil.

◆ Place in the grilling machine and grill 8 to 10 minutes until browned. Alternatively, cook on a preheated grill about 5 minutes on each side.

◆ Reheat sauce. Drizzle artichokes with remaining seasoned oil, garnish with parsley, and serve with red bell pepper sauce.

Spicy Potato, Shallot and Fennel Kabobs

MAKES 4 SERVINGS

*24 baby new potatoes
(about 1 pound in total weight)*

8 small shallots

*16 baby fennel bulbs,
(about 10 ounces in total weight)*

MARINADE

1 tablespoon mustard seeds

1 tablespoon cumin seeds

1 tablespoon garam masala

2 teaspoons turmeric

1 tablespoon lemon juice

½ cup peanut oil

Salt and ground black pepper

◆ Cook potatoes in boiling, salted water about 12 minutes until tender. Drain and transfer to a large mixing bowl to cool.

◆ Cook shallots in boiling water 4 minutes, drain, and, when cool enough to handle, peel them. Add to potatoes, along with fennel bulbs.

◆ To make the marinade, crush mustard and cumin seeds lightly and place them in a bowl with garam masala, turmeric, lemon juice, peanut oil, salt, and pepper. Stir to combine.

◆ Pour marinade over prepared vegetables and toss to coat well. Cover and refrigerate 2 hours, if time permits.

◆ Remove vegetables from spicy marinade and thread onto skewers.

◆ Place kabobs in the grilling machine and grill 7 or 8 minutes. Alternatively, cook on a preheated grill about 12 minutes, turning and basting with marinade while cooking.

Halloumi, Zucchini and Mushroom Skewers

MAKES 4 SERVINGS

12 ounces halloumi cheese

1 red bell pepper, halved, cored, and seeded

1 medium zucchini, cut into 8 chunks

8 large mushrooms, halved

½ cup extra virgin olive oil

2 tablespoons chopped fresh thyme

2 garlic cloves, chopped

ground black pepper

◆ Cut cheese and red bell pepper into 1-inch squares. Place them in a shallow dish with zucchini and mushrooms.

◆ In a small bowl, mix together olive oil, thyme, garlic, and ground black pepper and pour over vegetables. Toss gently to coat evenly.

◆ Thread cheese and vegetables on skewers. Place in the grilling machine and grill 5 or 6 minutes. Alternatively, cook skewers on a preheated grill about 8 minutes, turning occasionally and brushing with remaining oil mixture while cooking.

◆ Skewers are ready to serve when cheese is golden and vegetables are tender.

Fennel with Feta and Pears

MAKES 4 SERVINGS

2 FENNEL BULBS

¼ CUP OLIVE OIL

6 OUNCES FETA CHEESE

1 RIPE PEAR

4 SUN-DRIED TOMATOES IN OIL, DRAINED AND SLICED

8 PITTED BLACK OLIVES

1 TABLESPOON BASIL LEAVES, SHREDDED

1 TEASPOON LEMON JUICE

½ TEASPOON CLEAR HONEY

SALT AND GROUND BLACK PEPPER

◆ Trim fennel, discarding any damaged outer leaves. Cut each bulb lengthwise into 6 thin slices.

◆ Brush fennel slices with a little olive oil, place in the grilling machine, and grill 4 or 5 minutes until browned and just tender. Alternatively, cook on a preheated grill 2 or 3 minutes on each side. Let cool slightly.

◆ Slice feta into thin slabs. Quarter, core, and thinly slice pear. Arrange fennel, cheese, and pear on serving plates and top with sliced sun-dried tomatoes, olives, and shredded basil.

◆ Blend remaining oil, lemon juice, and honey together and season to taste. Drizzle dressing over salad and serve.

Carrot and Lentil Patties

MAKES 4 TO 6 SERVINGS

1¼ CUPS RED LENTILS

1 TABLESPOON OLIVE OIL

1 SMALL ONION, FINELY CHOPPED

8 OUNCES CARROTS, VERY FINELY CHOPPED

2 GARLIC CLOVES, FINELY CHOPPED

2 TEASPOONS CUMIN

½ TEASPOON CAYENNE

3 TABLESPOONS CHOPPED PARSLEY

½ CUP FRESH BREADCRUMBS

1 EGG, BEATEN

YOGURT SAUCE

SCANT 1 CUP PLAIN YOGURT

1 OR 2 GARLIC CLOVES, CRUSHED

1 TEASPOON LEMON JUICE

1 TABLESPOON CHOPPED PARSLEY

◆ Put lentils in a large pan of salted water, bring to a boil, then simmer 15 minutes until tender. Drain, put in a bowl and mash lightly.

◆ Heat oil, add onion and cook until golden. Add carrots and garlic and cook an additional 3 minutes. Stir in cumin and cayenne.

◆ Add carrot mixture to lentils and mix in parsley, breadcrumbs, and egg. Season with salt and pepper.

◆ Shape carrot and lentil mixture into 12 patties, place on a tray, and chill until ready to cook.

◆ To make sauce, combine yogurt, crushed garlic, lemon juice, and parsley in a bowl. Cover and refrigerate until required.

◆ Brush patties on both sides with oil. Place in the grilling machine and grill 5 to 7 minutes until golden brown. Alternatively, cook on a preheated grill about 3 or 4 minutes on each side until golden brown, turning carefully.

◆ Serve 2 or 3 patties to each person. Serve yogurt sauce separately.

Vegetable Kabobs with Cilantro Sauce

MAKES 4 SERVINGS

2 CORN-ON-THE-COB, SLICED INTO
¾-INCH ROUNDS

2 RED ONIONS, CUT INTO 3-LAYER
1-INCH PIECES

1 RED AND 1 YELLOW BELL PEPPER, SEEDED
AND CUT INTO 1-INCH PIECES

8 BABY PATTYPAN SQUASH, HALVED,
OR 2 SMALL ZUCCHINI, CUT INTO
½-INCH CHUNKS

16 SMALL SHIITAKE MUSHROOMS,
STEMS REMOVED

8 FIRM CHERRY TOMATOES

¾ STICK BUTTER

3 TABLESPOONS OLIVE OIL

1 GARLIC CLOVE,
VERY FINELY CHOPPED

½ TEASPOON CORIANDER SEEDS,
CRUSHED

PINCH CAYENNE

SALT AND PEPPER

CILANTRO SAUCE

2¼ CUPS CHOPPED FRESH
CILANTRO LEAVES

¾ CUP CHOPPED FLAT-LEAF PARSLEY

2 GREEN ONIONS, CHOPPED

1 GARLIC CLOVE, CRUSHED

2 TABLESPOONS LIME JUICE

1½ TEASPOONS TOASTED CUMIN SEEDS

¼ TEASPOON SALT

GROUND BLACK PEPPER, TO TASTE

⅓ CUP PLAIN YOGURT

⅓ CUP THICK CREAM

◆ Prepare corn, onions, bell peppers, pattypan squash, and mushrooms and thread onto 8 skewers with cherry tomatoes. Melt butter with olive oil, garlic, coriander seeds, cayenne, and salt and pepper. Brush the kabobs with the melted butter mixture.

◆ To make cilantro sauce, place cilantro, parsley, green onions, garlic, lime juice, cumin seeds, salt, and pepper in a food processor and purée 3 minutes, stopping to scrape the sides of the bowl frequently. Pour into a bowl and stir in yogurt and cream.

◆ Place kabobs in the grilling machine and grill 10 to 12 minutes until just tender and beginning to blacken around the edges. Alternatively, cook on a preheated grill about 15 minutes, turning and basting frequently. Serve kabobs with cilantro sauce.

Grilled Eggplant Salad

MAKES 4 SERVINGS

2 SMALL EGGPLANTS

1 RED ONION

⅓ CUP OLIVE OIL

¼ TEASPOON DRIED RED PEPPER FLAKES

½ TEASPOON CUMIN SEEDS

½ TEASPOON SESAME SEEDS

2 GARLIC CLOVES, VERY FINELY CHOPPED

BLACK PEPPER AND ¼ TEASPOON SALT

2 TABLESPOONS LIME JUICE

SLICES OF LIME AND CILANTRO LEAVES TO GARNISH

DRESSING

⅔ CUP PLAIN YOGURT

2 TABLESPOONS FINELY CHOPPED CILANTRO

GRATED ZEST ½ LIME

1 GARLIC CLOVE, VERY FINELY CHOPPED

SALT AND PEPPER

◆ Cut eggplant into ½-inch slices and onion into ¼-inch slices. Keep onion rings in one piece by inserting 2 toothpicks from outer ring to center. Put eggplant and onion slices in a large bowl.

◆ Combine olive oil, red pepper flakes, cumin and sesame seeds, garlic, salt, and pepper. Pour mixture over eggplant and onion slices, turning to coat. Marinate at least 30 minutes.

◆ Meanwhile, make dressing. Mix together yogurt, cilantro, lime zest, garlic, salt, and pepper. Let stand.

◆ Carefully remove eggplant and onion slices from marinade. Place in the grilling machine and grill eggplant slices 8 to 10 minutes and onion slices 5 or 6 minutes, until browned. Alternatively, cook vegetables on a preheated grill about 5 minutes on each side. Allow to cool.

◆ Remove toothpicks from onion slices and cut each slice in 4. Cut small eggplant slices in half and larger ones in 4.

◆ Mix onion and eggplant in a serving bowl and sprinkle with lime juice. Carefully fold in yogurt mixture. Leave at room temperature about 1 hour. Garnish with lime slices and cilantro leaves to serve.

Vegetable Kabobs with Red Bell Pepper Salsa

MAKES 4 SERVINGS

1 LARGE ZUCCHINI

16 SMALL FIRM TOMATOES

8 CHESTNUT MUSHROOMS

1 GREEN BELL PEPPER, SEEDED AND CUT INTO CHUNKS

1 YELLOW OR ORANGE BELL PEPPER, SEEDED AND CUT INTO CHUNKS

8 BABY ONIONS, OR 2 SMALL ONIONS, QUARTERED

3 TABLESPOONS OLIVE OIL

3 GARLIC CLOVES, CRUSHED

1 TABLESPOON LEMON JUICE

½ TEASPOON DRIED THYME

RED BELL PEPPER SALSA

2 RED BELL PEPPERS, SEEDED AND ROUGHLY CHOPPED

3 TABLESPOONS OLIVE OIL

3 GARLIC CLOVES

1 TABLESPOON RED WINE VINEGAR

8 SUN-DRIED TOMATOES IN OIL, DRAINED

1 SMALL RED ONION, ROUGHLY CHOPPED

2 TABLESPOONS CHOPPED PARSLEY

◆ Halve zucchini lengthwise and cut into ½-inch slices. Thread onto skewers with tomatoes, mushrooms, chunks of green and yellow bell pepper, and onions. Place skewers on a large serving plate or tray.

◆ In a small bowl, mix together olive oil, garlic, lemon juice, and thyme. Brush over vegetable kabobs.

◆ To make salsa, put red peppers in a blender or food processor with oil, garlic, vinegar, sun-dried tomatoes, and onion. Blend until very finely chopped. Season and add parsley.

◆ Place kabobs in the grilling machine and grill 8 to 10 minutes. Alternatively, cook on a preheated grill 10 to 15 minutes, turning and brushing with baste occasionally.

◆ Serve hot vegetable kabobs with red bell pepper salsa.

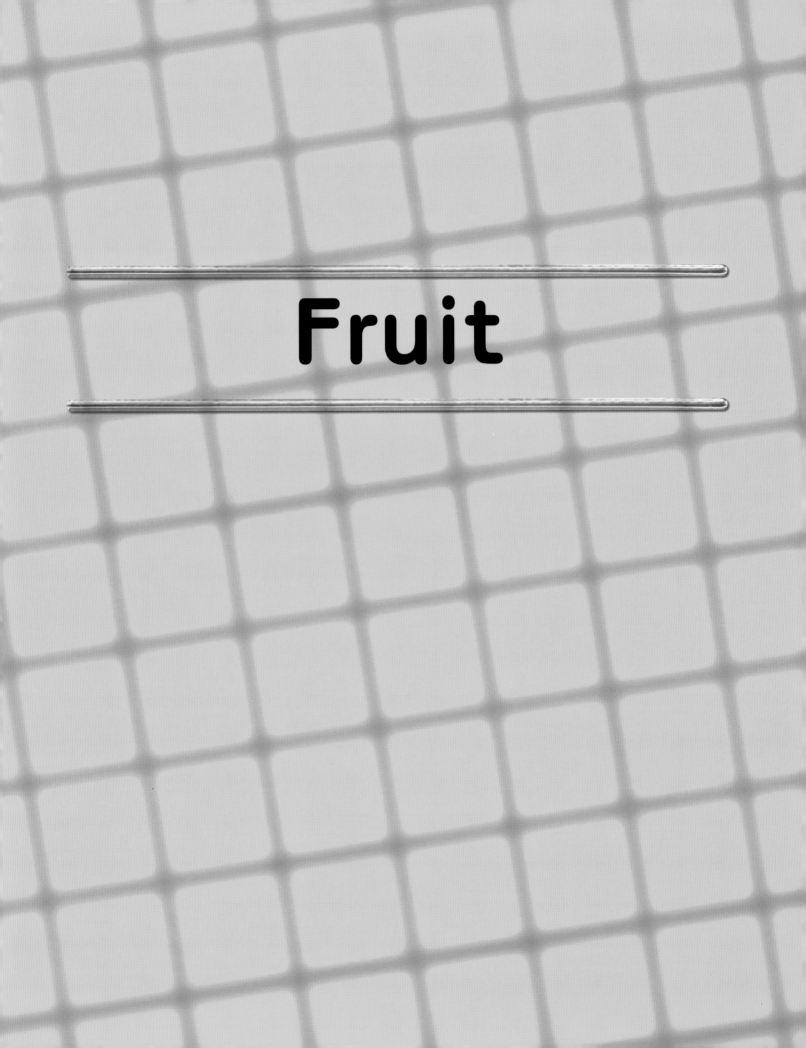

Fruit

Exotic Fruit with Passion Fruit Dip

1 SMALL RIPE MANGO

2 BANANAS

2 THICK SLICES FRESH PINEAPPLE, HALVED

1 SMALL RIPE PAW PAW

½ STICK UNSALTED BUTTER, MELTED

2 TEASPOONS CONFECTIONERS' SUGAR, SIFTED

PASSION FRUIT DIP

SCANT 1 CUP THICK SOUR CREAM

1 TABLESPOON CONFECTIONERS' SUGAR, SIFTED

PULP AND JUICE 3 PASSION FRUIT

MINT SPRIGS, TO DECORATE

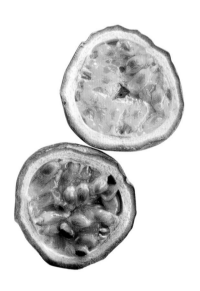

◆ To make dip, mix together in a bowl thick sour cream, confectioners' sugar, and passion fruit pulp and juice. Cover and refrigerate.

◆ Cut mango into quarters around the pit. Halve bananas lengthwise, but do not peel. Cut paw paw into 4 thick slices and seed.

◆ Place paw paw and pineapple slices, mango quarters and banana halves on a large tray. Mix together melted butter and confectioners' sugar, and brush mixture all over fruit.

◆ Place mango, pineapple, and bananas in the grilling machine and cook 2 or 3 minutes. Add paw paw and cook an additional 2 minutes.

Alternatively, place mango, pineapple, and bananas on a baking tray on a preheated grill and cook 2 minutes. Add paw paw and cook an additional 4 minutes, turning occasionally.

◆ Garnish with mint sprigs and serve fruit with dip.

Figs with Cinnamon Cream

MAKES 6 SERVINGS

9 LARGE RIPE FIGS

½ STICK UNSALTED BUTTER

4 TEASPOONS BRANDY

3 TEASPOONS BROWN SUGAR

SLIVERED ALMONDS, TO DECORATE

CINNAMON CREAM

⅔ CUP THICK CREAM

1 TEASPOON GROUND CINNAMON

1 TABLESPOON BRANDY

2 TEASPOONS CLEAR HONEY

◆ To make cinnamon cream, in a small bowl, combine cream, ground cinnamon, brandy, and honey. Cover and refrigerate for 30 minutes to allow flavors to develop.

◆ Halve figs and thread onto 6 skewers. Melt butter in a small pan and stir in brandy. Brush figs with brandy butter and sprinkle with sugar.

◆ Place skewers in the grilling machine and grill 3 or 4 minutes until bubbling and golden. Alternatively, cook on a preheated grill 4 or 5 minutes.

◆ Whip cinnamon cream until just holding its shape and serve with grilled figs, decorated with slivered almonds.

Fruit Skewers with Chocolate Nut Sauce

MAKES 6 SERVINGS

12 STRAWBERRIES

6 APRICOTS, HALVED

*3 PEARS, PEELED AND
CUT INTO QUARTERS*

*2 TABLESPOONS SUPERFINE
GRANULATED SUGAR*

CHOCOLATE NUT SAUCE

*4 OUNCES SEMISWEET CHOCOLATE,
CHOPPED*

⅔ CUP LIGHT CREAM

6 MARSHMALLOWS, CHOPPED

*3 TABLESPOONS SKINLESS HAZELNUTS,
TOASTED AND CHOPPED*

◆ To make sauce, melt chocolate, cream, and marshmallows in a saucepan over low heat, stirring continuously. Whisk until smooth, then boil 2 minutes to thicken. Stir in nuts and set sauce aside.

◆ Place strawberries, apricots, and pears in a bowl, sprinkle over sugar and toss gently to coat. Divide fruit between skewers.

◆ Place fruit skewers in the grilling machine and grill 4 or 5 minutes until fruit is warmed through. Alternatively, cook on a preheated grill 5 or 6 minutes, turning frequently.

◆ Serve hot with chocolate nut sauce passed separately for dipping.

Bananas with Maple Syrup and Pecan Nuts

MAKES 4 SERVINGS

4 BANANAS

*½ CUP PECAN NUTS,
COARSELY CHOPPED*

⅓ CUP MAPLE SYRUP

*VANILLA OR RUM AND RAISIN
ICE CREAM, TO SERVE (OPTIONAL)*

◆ Place unpeeled bananas in the grilling machine and cook 10 to 12 minutes, until skins are completely black and bananas soft. Alternatively, cook on a preheated grill 12 to 15 minutes, turning frequently.

◆ Just before serving, gently warm pecan nuts and maple syrup in a saucepan over low heat.

◆ To serve, remove bananas from their skins and top with warm nutty syrup. Serve with scoops of ice cream, if desired.